# TURKISH KALEIDOSCOPE

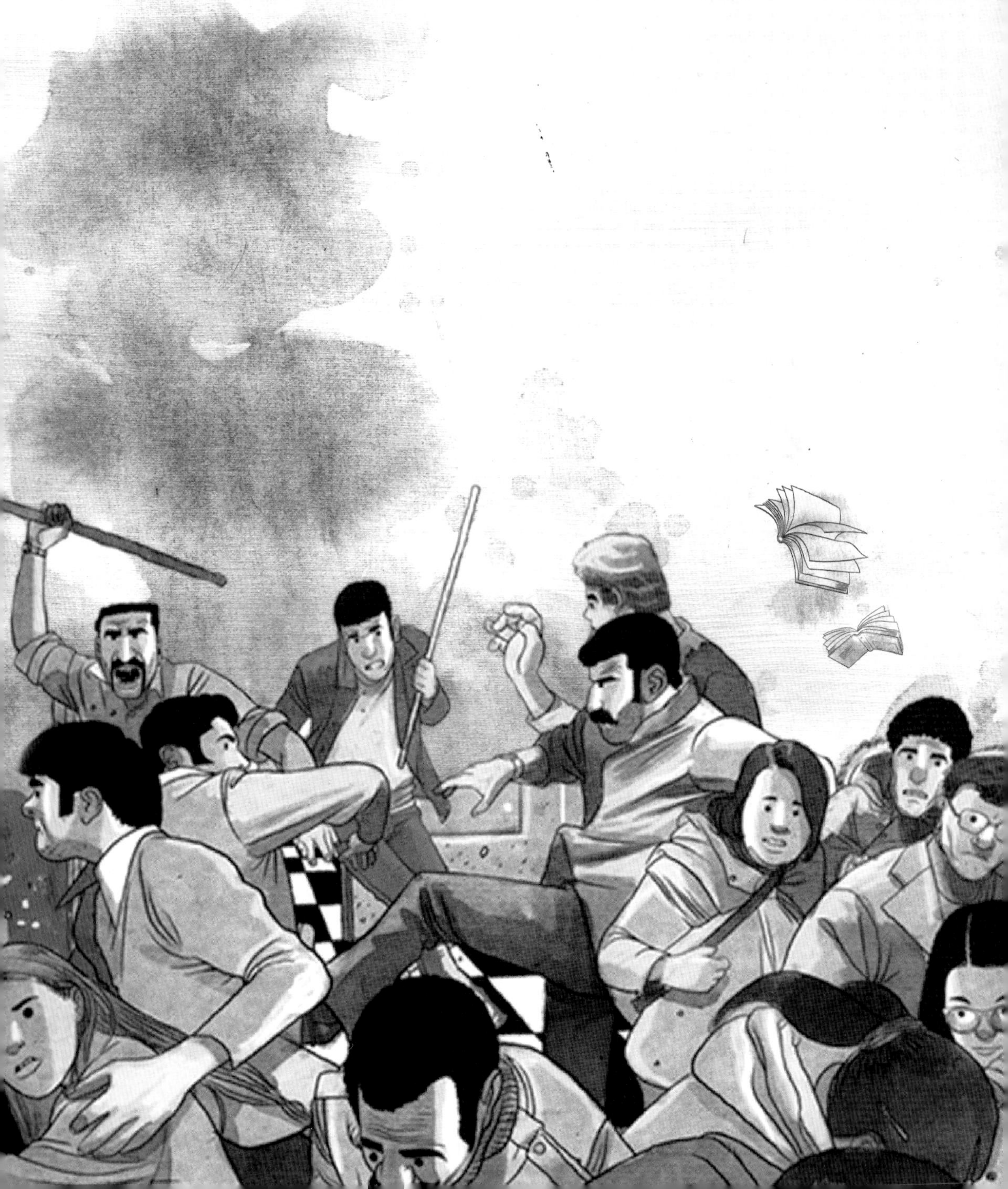

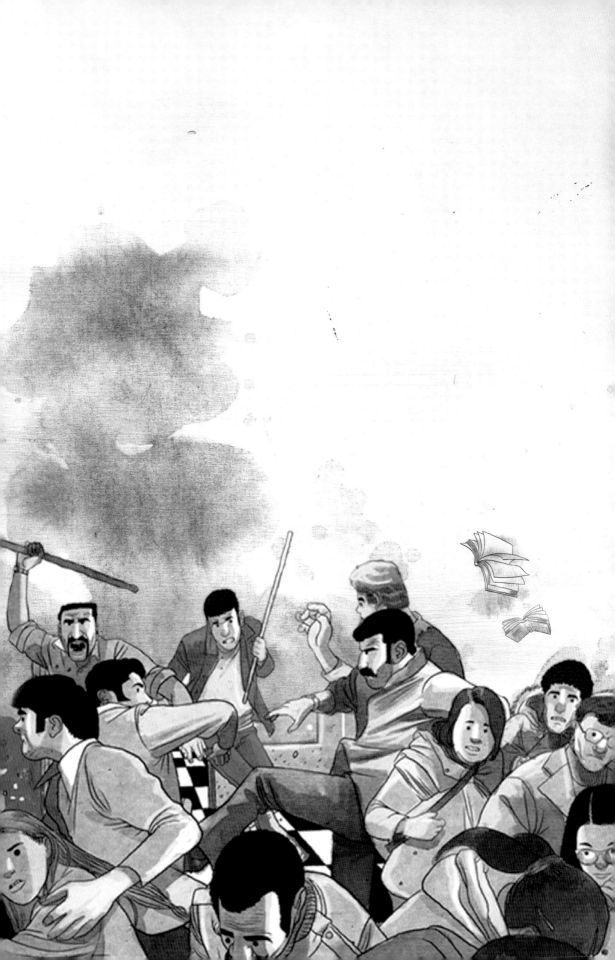

# TURKISH
# KALEIDOSCOPE

## FRACTURED LIVES IN A TIME OF VIOLENCE

## STORY BY JENNY WHITE
## ART BY ERGÜN GÜNDÜZ

PRINCETON UNIVERSITY PRESS
Princeton and Oxford

Requests for permission to reproduce material from this work
should be sent to permissions@press.princeton.edu

Published by Princeton University Press
41 William Street, Princeton, New Jersey 08540
6 Oxford Street, Woodstock, Oxfordshire OX20 1TR

press.princeton.edu

ISBN (pbk.) 978-0-691-20519-9
ISBN (e-book) 978-0-691-21549-5

British Library Cataloging-in-Publication Data is available

Editorial: Fred Appel and Jenny Tan
Production Editorial: Mark Bellis
Text and Cover Design: Jessica Massabrook
Lettering: Veli Okulan
Production: Steve Sears
Publicity: Kate Hensley and Kathryn Stevens
Cover Credit: Ergün Gündüz

This book has been composed in Countach & Sabon LT Std

Printed on acid-free paper. ∞

Printed in Korea

1  3  5  7  9  10  8  6  4  2

Inside a kaleidoscope, two or more mirrors tilted at angles reflect each other. When you look into one end of the tube at an object before you, the object you observe has been repeatedly reflected and appears to your eye as a fractured, symmetrical pattern. At the far end, the tube often contains loose, colored pieces of glass that tumble about when rotated, so their colors and patterns are reflected into the image, creating a regular, but ever-changing, view.

# INTRODUCTION

In 1975, I traveled from the East Coast of the United States to Turkey's capital city, Ankara, to begin studying at Hacettepe University for a master's degree in social psychology. I was interested in cross-cultural psychology and the university had an impressive program. With the help of a few friends, I settled in to study and learn the language. In those pre-Internet days, I had no idea that the country (and my university) was embroiled in what might be called a civil war. I learned quickly enough. In the simple everyday act of attending class, I encountered armored personnel carriers, bullets, bombs, and other dangers. Between 1976 and 1980, five thousand civilians were killed in street violence. By the time I left in 1978, the polarization and fury of street violence between groups professing "leftist" and "rightist" views had enveloped nearly the entire country and affected young and old. The violence accompanied tremendous economic hardship and political dysfunction. For most of that decade, no political party had an absolute majority, so the country was governed by a series of unstable coalitions. Whenever the coalition cards were shuffled, the parties that came out on top rewarded themselves with cabinet posts and ministries that they colonized by replacing thousands of civil servants with party loyalists. Before long, another set of parties aligned themselves at the top and did the same. In this kaleidoscope of ideologically opposed coalition governments, each ministry operated against the others at all levels of society, so that a change in ideological leadership at the ministry level would result in a wholesale swap from leftist to rightist and back again in every linked institution. When the Ministry of Education was occupied by rightists, leftist teachers were replaced or attacked and the men who brought tea to university offices suddenly began to carry clubs and intimidate leftist students. Political participation, willing or unwilling, was widespread, drawing in people of all ages and in every corner of the country. Urban neighborhoods were controlled by one group or another and marked with graffiti and posters that identified their territory. Before long, there were parallel police forces and parallel governments; even the army was split.

The left-right axis of polarization infected not only Turkey but many other countries during this period. The Cold War was a battle for global supremacy between the Soviet Union and the United States using proxies, countries that they tried to influence. The left/right dualism, however, is misleading. Communism came in Sovietic, Albanian, Maoist, and Cuban flavors; there were different types of socialism, and other even narrower splinter positions, groups that had split over personal affronts, matters of honor, or simply disagreement about how to interpret a line in *The Communist Manifesto*. By 1980, there were more than fifty leftist groups operating in Turkey. The consequences were serious as groups often dueled in the streets with guns and other weapons. The right was divided between Turanist nationalists who believed Turks had a common ancestry in Central Asia, symbolized by a wolf, and by Islamist nationalists who foregrounded Islamic identity and Turkish blood. However, these beliefs overlapped and, despite some internal disputes, the wrath of rightist groups focused firmly on the left. Many Alevis, a large Muslim minority whose rituals and beliefs differ substantially from those of majority Sunni Muslims, were associated with the left. This made them particular targets of rightist bombings and drive-by shootings.

During this period, Turkey experienced massive migration as peasants looked for jobs in the factories springing up around the cities. Peasants and workers built illegal houses on public or unused land until almost a third of Turkey's major cities consisted of such squatter areas. These migrants tended to be conservative in lifestyle, though their level of religious piety varied. The left tried to organize them, but they gravitated to the political right. Turks with a secular lifestyle, ranging from factory workers and artisans to educated elites, tended toward the political left. Many would have liked to remain in a political middle, but this was no longer an option. With the possible exception of the bohemians, these seemingly opposed populations still had a great deal in common, including a basic conservatism about women's proper role in society, respect for authority that expressed itself both in family life and hierarchies of political organization, and strong nationalist beliefs, including veneration of the country's founder, Mustafa Kemal Ataturk, and a belief in Kemalist principles. Ataturk was one of the heroes of Turkey's War of Independence from occupying European powers in World War I and Turkey's first president. In his own autocratic way, he pushed through many Westernizing reforms and gave Turkey a parliament.

In 1973, an international oil crisis raised prices beyond what Turkey was able to pay, leading to shortages and strikes. An international arms embargo in 1975 in response to Turkey's invasion of Cyprus pushed Turkey's economy over the edge. At first, imported goods like coffee and medicines disappeared from the market. Then local basics, like cooking oil, began to disappear from grocery shelves. Fuel was not available to truck coal from the mines to the cities, leaving people to burn their furniture to keep warm. Electricity and water were supplied only a few hours a day. As the kaleidoscope of political coalitions spun ineffectively in parliament, the Turkish military readied a takeover. The coup d'état in 1980 replaced street violence with the more efficient violence of the state that brutally repressed activists, particularly on the left, though rightists also were rounded up. More than two hundred thousand people were arrested, many were tortured, some were executed. Hundreds of thousands of others were stripped of their citizenship, blacklisted, or simply disappeared. Those who could, fled abroad.

In 1983, the army allowed new elections. A civilian government came to power that prioritized economic reforms and opened Turkey to the global market. New consumer products and hopes for upward mobility gripped Turkey's population and the extreme polarization and violent turn in the 1970s were largely repressed. People wanted to forget, though their experiences were transmitted to the next generation in indirect ways. The military presented itself as the protector of Kemalism, that is, the secular society and parliamentary government envisioned by Ataturk, but in the

1980s, it also began to promote Islam as the glue that could challenge the appeal of communism and heal the rifts in society. The newly elected government introduced compulsory religious education and increased the public role of religion. Still, beneath the gleaming new society, a steady drumbeat of violence persisted, most visibly in the fight between the Turkish state and the PKK (Kurdistan Workers' Party), a revolutionary socialist organization that has survived to the present day. It has roots in the leftist movement of the late 1970s and then, in the 1980s, began an armed insurgency to establish a separate Kurdish state and to safeguard the rights of Turkey's Kurdish population. More than forty thousand people have been killed in decades of conflict between the PKK and the state, most of them Kurds.

Today, Turkey is again experiencing extreme polarization, though the social and political context and labels identifying opposing "sides" differ from the 1970s. Since the early Republic, women wearing headscarves were banned from the civil service, parliament, hospitals, and many other kinds of employment and, for a time, from attending university. People with a conservative lifestyle felt left out of the secular Kemalist national project and supported new Islamist political parties that promised to give them a place at the table. The election of the AKP (Justice and Development Party) in 2002 under its charismatic leader, Recep Tayyip Erdoğan, seemed at first to promise a table big enough for everyone.

Other doors to conservative success were opened by Hizmet, the Islamic community surrounding the preacher Fethullah Gülen, which operated schools and businesses, funded civic activities, and filled positions in the civil service. In 2015, the government designated Hizmet as a terror organization with the acronym FETÖ (Fethullahist Terrorist Organization), accusing it of setting up a parallel state within Turkey, and began to arrest anyone with links to the community. The government believed FETÖ was behind a failed coup attempt in 2016. Since then, the accusation of being FETÖ or PKK (or, implausibly, both) has become generic for "terrorist" and resulted in tens of thousands of people in all walks of life being fired from their positions, detained, or imprisoned. The government encouraged citizens to denounce to the police anyone they suspected of supporting either group.

Mutual suspicion and distrust reached a fever pitch. Everyone claimed a bitterly defended side, but the boundaries between "us" and "them" were constantly moving. In 2017, voters approved a referendum to replace Turkey's parliamentary system with a new constellation of power that revolved around a strong presidency rather than parliament. The following year, Erdoğan was voted in as president under this new system and fully gathered in the reins of power. By 2019, though, fractures in the ruling party started to appear as several prominent former supporters of the president stepped forward to start their own political parties.

Given this background, I thought the story behind Turkey's polarization in the 1970s might be important for understanding today's dynamics. I began this project because I saw that, after four decades of near silence (with the exception of Cold War–themed ideological analyses and a handful of memoirs), the 1970s were suddenly being recast in Turkish popular media and incorporated into television series, sometimes in ways that I didn't recognize. In 2012, two generals who led the 1980 coup were brought to trial and the court heard testimony by the victims of the coup, but their stories began where the 1970s left off. If a social history of the period leading up to the coup is to be written, I thought it should reflect the voices and experiences of ordinary people as much as movement leaders, and those on the right as well as the left. This book lays out the personal motivations and actions of a variety of ordinary people who were directly or indirectly involved in the rightist and leftist activism that ensnared a large part of the population in the 1970s. Some of the scenes in this book are from my own experience, but most of the stories are inspired by dozens of interviews I carried out in Turkey in 2014 with a wide variety of people who participated in the fury of that period.

In the interviews, certain themes emerged, regardless of the ideological position (left or right), gender, social class, ethnic or religious affiliation, or rural/urban characteristics of the speaker. For instance, people joined political groups for many different reasons, not all of them political. When they joined a group, every aspect of their lives was controlled by an autocratic leader. There was no room for complexity or personal choice. A person's political affiliation could even be read from their clothing and shape of their facial hair. Women were expected to be asexual soldiers, but also to bring the tea. There was a lack of trust in individuals and no tolerance whatsoever for thinking or behaving differently. Agreement with and obedience to the leader were paramount.

Despite such intense conformity within rigidly autocratic hierarchies, I was struck by the tendency for Turkish political life at the time, as now, to polarize and fracture into violently antagonistic groups and sides. Members of the left, in particular, carried out violent acts against competing leftist groups, even if they were ideologically similar. Those who abandoned their group were considered traitors and met with intense hatred. Their own group might send an assassin to kill them. At the microlevel, people's stories show that, within the suffocating embrace of group membership, a variety of motivations and experiences led people to rethink their affiliation to a particular person or position, despite the risk.

Why a graphic novel? When doing the interviews, I had no specific agenda and allowed myself to be surprised by people's stories and motivations. People's memories of the time were vivid and often they seemed to relive their experiences in the telling. It occurred to me that academic analysis flattened these stories as it folded them into discussions of abstract issues, like factionalism. Perhaps I could make the same points by allowing people to tell their stories themselves in graphic form and thereby retain the nuances and contradictions of history as it is lived. We can analyze data and build models to try to explain the origins of factionalism and descent into political violence, but the reality always involves complexities of real actors negotiating cultural, social, and historical pressures. A graphic novel explains the same things in a more subtle way by embedding them within highly evocative life experiences, personal turning points, and coming-of-age stories. In order to produce an engaging dramatic narrative, I had to create composite characters, merge their stories, and fictionalize their relationships, making this a work of graphic fiction based on true stories. Although I've written both scholarly books and novels, this was a new and unfamiliar endeavor. The success of this project depended greatly on the talented artist Ergün Gündüz, who was sensitive to these nuances, could evoke Turkey in the 1970s, and had the patience of a dervish. After reading my first lengthy text, he explained kindly, "I can't draw what's in people's heads," then taught me to write what is essentially a screenplay for a graphic book. I flew regularly to Istanbul and we would sit for many hours at a stretch, going over every word and deciding whether and how it would be drawn, inserted into a speech bubble, or omitted. In this way, the book before you took shape over many iterations, countless hours of mulling over words and images, and always a concern to be faithful to the original telling.

This book doesn't give an ideological or event-driven analysis but rather asks more universal questions about what causes people to sacrifice their lives, health, and sometimes families for a cause or for an autocratic leader, to engage in violent acts, and then to endanger themselves further by splitting off from that cause or leader. What effect, if any, do their actions have on their society, on their own lives and those of their children? From the vantage point of people on the ground, these questions take on a universal quality that speaks to other contexts and other people beyond Turkey and beyond the 1970s.

*"There are stories that open many veins."*
**INTERVIEWEE 1**

*"Anything can happen to anyone at any time."*
**INTERVIEWEE 2**

# ACKNOWLEDGMENTS

I would like to thank Riksbankens Jubileumsfond, Stockholm University Department of Asian, Middle Eastern and Turkish Studies, and the Stockholm University Institute for Turkish Studies for making it possible to research, write, and draw this book with their generous funding and support. The Swedish Institute in Istanbul provided logistical support. I am grateful to the many kind people who were willing to share their stories with me; I hope I do them justice. I am indebted to our supportive department staff and to my colleagues and friends who introduced me around, read drafts and checked their accuracy, and helped me figure out how to do this new thing, a graphic book! I would particularly like to thank Fred Appel, our enormously helpful and ever patient editor at Princeton University Press. Above all, I am indebted to Ergün Gündüz, without whom this book would never have happened, for sharing his enormous talent and enthusiasm, and for working patiently through endless revisions. And to Lars, who saw the first stick figures I drew and still believed it would happen.

# INCOMPLETE GLOSSARY OF FACTIONS AND PARTIES

---

FETÖ: Fethullahist Terrorist Organization

## ON THE RIGHT
AKP: Justice and Development Party
Gray Wolves: Idealist Hearths
MHP: Nationalist Movement Party
POL-BIR: The Police Union
ÜGB: Idealist Youth Union

## ON THE LEFT
DAZ: Revolutionary Morality Police
Dev-Genç: Revolutionary Youth Federation of Turkey
Dev-Sol: Revolutionary Left
Dev-Yol: Revolutionary Path
DHKP-C: Revolutionary People's Liberation Party/Front
DISK: Revolutionary Workers' Trade Unions Confederation
DÖB: Revolutionary Students Union
GSB: Young Socialists Union
IGD: Progressive Youth Association
IKD: Progressive Women's Association
PKK: Kurdistan Workers' Party
POL-DER: The Police Association
SGB: Socialist Youth Union
SIP: Socialist Workers Party
TDK: Revolutionary Women's Union of Turkey
THKO: People's Liberation Army of Turkey
THKP: People's Liberation Party of Turkey
THKP-C: People's Liberation Party/Front of Turkey
TIIKP: Revolutionary Workers' and Peasants' Party of Turkey
TIP: Turkish Workers Party
TKP: Turkish Communist Party

# CAST OF CHARACTERS

———

Rightists referred to themselves as idealists (*ülkücü*). The left called them fascists. Leftists were self-defined revolutionaries (*devrimciler*). The right called them communists.

## MAIN CHARACTERS

Faruk,
Rightist

Nuray,
Leftist

Yunus,
Leftist

Orhan,
Rightist

## THEIR CHILDREN

Ebru,
Faruk's daughter

Eylem,
daughter of
Nuray & Yunus

Alp,
Orhan's son

Miray,
Orhan's
daughter

# SECONDARY CHARACTERS

Bilge,
Nuray's sister

Feride,
Nuray's friend

Fikret,
Nuray's brother

Gül,
Bilge's friend

# PERIPHERAL CHARACTERS

Ali,
bakery worker

Metin,
Fikret's friend

Mustafa,
leader of
Yunus's
leftist group

Mehmet,
electrical shop
owner

Sedef,
Yunus's
great aunt

The factory
owner

Yunus's
uncle

# TURKISH KALEIDOSCOPE

# REFLECTIONS

## Faruk

FARUK WAS BORN IN ERZURUM, THE YOUNGEST OF THREE CHILDREN. HIS FATHER WAS A TINSMITH WHO OWNED A SHOP IN THE BAZAAR. BOTH OF HIS PARENTS WERE RELIGIOUS AND CONSERVATIVE IN THEIR VALUES AND LIFESTYLE. FOR FARUK, THAT MEANT THEY BELIEVED IN THE IMPORTANCE OF FAMILY, RESPECTFUL BEHAVIOR, KINDNESS, AND PRAYER. FARUK WAS DEEPLY IMPRESSED BY HIS FATHER, WHO OPENED THE DOOR TO HIS SHOP EVERY DAY WITH A PRAYER, THEN RECEIVED FORMAL GREETINGS FROM THE OTHER SHOPKEEPERS. THE FAMILY BELIEVED IN THE GREATNESS OF THE TURKISH NATION, A NATION OF WARRIORS WHO BEAT BACK EVERY THREAT BY OUTSIDERS. FARUK'S ELDER BROTHER BECAME A COMMANDO AND FARUK WISHED TO DO THE SAME, BUT HIS FATHER WANTED HIM TO TAKE OVER THE SHOP, MARRY, AND GIVE HIM GRANDSONS. AS A DUTIFUL SON, FARUK WOULDN'T DISOBEY HIS FATHER, BUT HE WAS ABLE TO SIDESTEP HIS FATHER'S PLAN BY WINNING A PLACE AT HACETTEPE UNIVERSITY TO STUDY MEDICINE. THERE HE LIVED HIS DREAM OF BEING A WARRIOR FOR THE NATION BY JOINING THE GRAY WOLVES YOUTH GROUP AND FIGHTING COMMUNISTS. HE BECAME BEST FRIENDS WITH ORHAN, ANOTHER STUDENT FROM ERZURUM.

## Nuray

WHEN NURAY WAS BORN, HER FATHER HAD QUIT HIS JOB AT A FACTORY AND MOVED HIS FAMILY BACK TO HIS FATHER'S VILLAGE TO HELP HIM WORK THE LAND. SHE HAD TWO OLDER SIBLINGS, BILGE AND FIKRET, WHO BOTH LEFT TO STUDY IN ISTANBUL. TO MAKE SURE THAT NURAY HAD A CHANCE AT A GOOD EDUCATION, THE FAMILY MOVED TO THE CITY OF ESKIŞEHIR, WHERE HER FATHER FOUND WORK. IN HIGH SCHOOL, HER TEACHERS GAVE HER BOOKS ABOUT OPPRESSION AND REVOLUTION. SHE IDOLIZED BILGE'S FRIEND GÜL, A UNION ORGANIZER. ALONG WITH ANOTHER STUDENT, YUNUS, NURAY BECAME INVOLVED IN A LEFTIST ORGANIZATION, KEEPING IT SECRET FROM HER PARENTS. SHE DID WELL ENOUGH ON THE NATIONAL ENTRANCE EXAMINATION TO STUDY MEDICINE AT HACETTEPE UNIVERSITY IN THE CAPITAL CITY OF ANKARA. HER EXPERIENCES THERE MADE HER MORE AND MORE SKEPTICAL ABOUT THE LEFTIST CAUSE. IN THE DORMITORY, SHE BEFRIENDED FERIDE, A YOUNG WOMAN FROM ADANA WHO WAS ALSO STUDYING MEDICINE.

# REFLECTIONS

## Yunus

YUNUS'S FAMILY IN ESKIŞEHIR HAD FALLEN ON HARD TIMES WHEN HIS FATHER, A TEACHER, WAS IMPRISONED. HIS MOTHER EARNED MONEY BY STITCHING AND SEWING. YUNUS HELPED NEIGHBORS WITH THE HARVEST IN RETURN FOR FOOD. HE MADE FRIENDS EASILY, BOTH IN ESKIŞEHIR AND WHEN HE WENT TO ANKARA TO STUDY, WHERE HE KEPT IN TOUCH WITH NURAY. AT HOME, YUNUS HAD ACCESS TO HIS FATHER'S MANY BOOKS AND HIS READING LED HIM TO BECOME A MARXIST. THE SUMMER BEFORE HE STARTED MEDICAL SCHOOL AT HACETTEPE UNIVERSITY, HE STAYED WITH HIS WEALTHY GREAT-AUNT SEDEF IN ANKARA. HER SON, YUNUS'S UNCLE, HAD JUST RETURNED FROM YEARS WORKING IN FRANCE. EVEN THOUGH YUNUS WAS DEEPLY COMMITTED TO THE LEFTIST CAUSE, HIS CONVERSATIONS WITH HIS UNCLE AND THE BOOKS HE GAVE YUNUS TO READ MADE HIM RECONSIDER WHAT TURKEY REALLY NEEDED.

## Orhan

ORHAN WAS A SHY YOUNG MAN FROM A CONSERVATIVE FAMILY IN ERZURUM. HIS FATHER MANAGED A SMALL FRUIT AND VEGETABLE SHOP. HE HAD TWO SISTERS. HIS MOTHER FINISHED THIRD GRADE BUT WANTED HER DAUGHTERS TO DO BETTER. HIS FAMILY WASN'T PARTICULARLY RELIGIOUS BUT HELD STRONGLY TO TRADITIONAL VALUES. ORHAN'S IDEAL VISION OF HIMSELF WAS AS A PHYSICIAN DOING GOOD IN THE WORLD, MARRIED TO A WOMAN HE LOVED, AND WITH CHILDREN OF HIS OWN. HE CONSIDERED HIMSELF TO BE A NATIONALIST IN THAT HE FELT HE BELONGED TO A NATIONAL COMMUNITY THAT CARED FOR AND PROTECTED ALL ITS CITIZENS, NO MATTER WHO THEY WERE. HE WAS NOT IN THE LEAST INTERESTED IN IDEOLOGY OR VIOLENCE; HE JUST WANTED TO FINISH HIS EDUCATION. HIS FRIEND FARUK, THOUGHT HIM NAIVE AND TRIED TO ENGAGE HIM IN A LARGER CAUSE.

1975, Ankara. Hacettepe University

## Orhan
# THE ROMANTIC

WHAT CLASS ARE YOU STUDYING FOR, SISTER?

CELL SCIENCES.

ME TOO. I HAVEN'T SEEN YOU IN CLASS. I'M ORHAN.

I TIED YOUR BLOND HAIR TO MY CRAZY HEART; IT CAN'T BE UNTANGLED, MIHRIBAN.*

I'M NURAY.

* MIHRIBAN: FOLK SONG ABOUT A ROMANTIC ANATOLIAN YOUTH WHO PUT TRADITIONAL VALUES AND FAMILY ABOVE HIS OWN DESIRES. HE LOVED MIHRIBAN BUT WAS TOO SHY TO TELL HER. SHE WAITED YEARS, THEN MARRIED SOMEONE ELSE.

YOU LIKE THAT GIRL. SHE'S A COMMUNIST. THEIR GIRLS DON'T HAVE MORALS.

DON'T TALK LIKE THAT ABOUT HER.

YOU'RE SUCH A ROMANTIC. WHY DON'T YOU JOIN OUR IDEALIST HEARTH?* YOU KNOW ALL THE BROTHERS AT THE DORMITORY. COME TO OUR MEETING TONIGHT. THERE'S A LECTURE ABOUT OUR GREAT TURKISH NATIONAL HISTORY.

LOOK, I LOVE MY HOMELAND AS MUCH AS ANYONE ELSE, BUT I BELIEVE IN THE VALUES OF MY FAMILY, NOT IN SOMEONE'S IDEOLOGY. DON'T YOU WANT TO GET MARRIED AND HAVE A FAMILY?

THAT'S WHAT MY FATHER WANTS, THAT I RETURN TO ERZURUM AND GIVE HIM GRANDSONS. FOR ME, THOUGH, THE MOVEMENT COMES FIRST. A WIFE WOULD JUST BE WAITING AT THE PRISON DOOR OR WEEPING OVER MY GRAVE.

WELL, WHAT DO YOU WANT IN LIFE?

SAME AS YOU, TO PROTECT OUR STATE AND OUR VALUES. IS YOUR FAMILY RELIGIOUS?

NOT REALLY.

* IDEALIST HEARTHS, ALSO KNOWN AS THE GRAY WOLVES, REFERS TO AN ULTRANATIONALIST YOUTH ORGANIZATION ASSOCIATED WITH THE ULTRANATIONALIST MHP (NATIONALIST MOVEMENT PARTY).

ALL WE WANT IS TO TURN TURKEY INTO A STRONG, DEVELOPED COUNTRY THAT HAS HONORED STATUS AMONG WORLD NATIONS LIKE IT USED TO. BUT RUSSIA, CHINA, FRANCE, THEY INJECT US WITH FOREIGN IDEAS AND MAKE OUR KIDS SHOOT EACH OTHER.

IT'S OUR OBLIGATION TO FIGHT BACK.

THE LEFTISTS CLAIM THEY'RE FIGHTING IMPERIALISM.

THEY THINK SO, BUT THEY'RE ACTUALLY TOOLS OF IMPERIALISM. OUR ENEMIES WANT TO CREATE ANARCHY, COLLAPSE THE SYSTEM, THEN SEIZE IT.

BROTHER, YOU SHOULDN'T BE SOME OTHER PERSON'S MAN.

BEING A NATIONALIST DOESN'T MAKE ME AGAINST ANYONE. I'M NOT RIGHT OR LEFT. IT MEANS FEELING THAT YOU BELONG. IT'S A POSITIVE THING.

YOU IDIOT. THEN BOTH SIDES WILL BEAT YOU UP. WHO'S GOING TO PROTECT YOU?

THE NEXT DAY IN CLASS.

DON'T GO IN THERE. WE'RE GOING TO RAID THEM.

SHOULD I LEAVE?

NO, JUST STAND HERE WITH US.

21

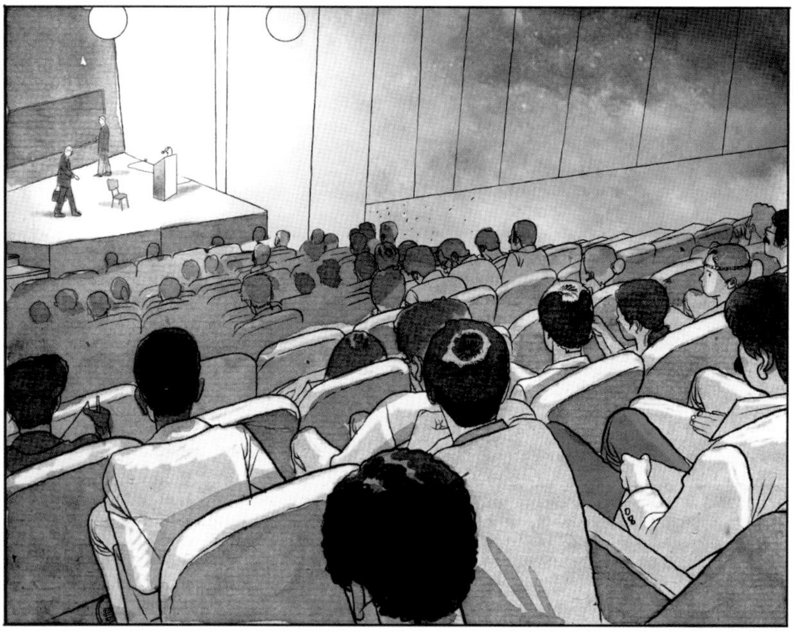

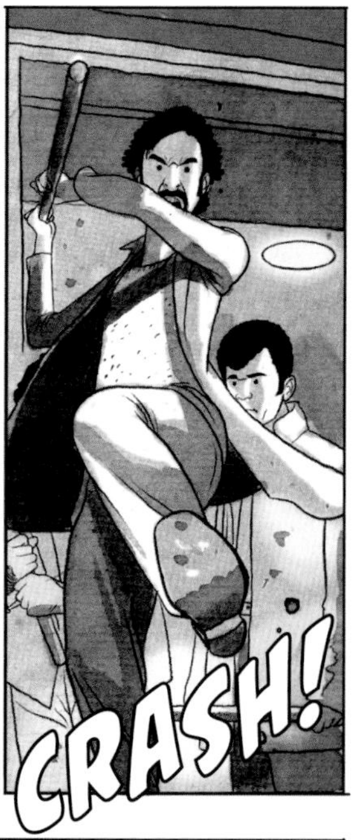
CRASH!

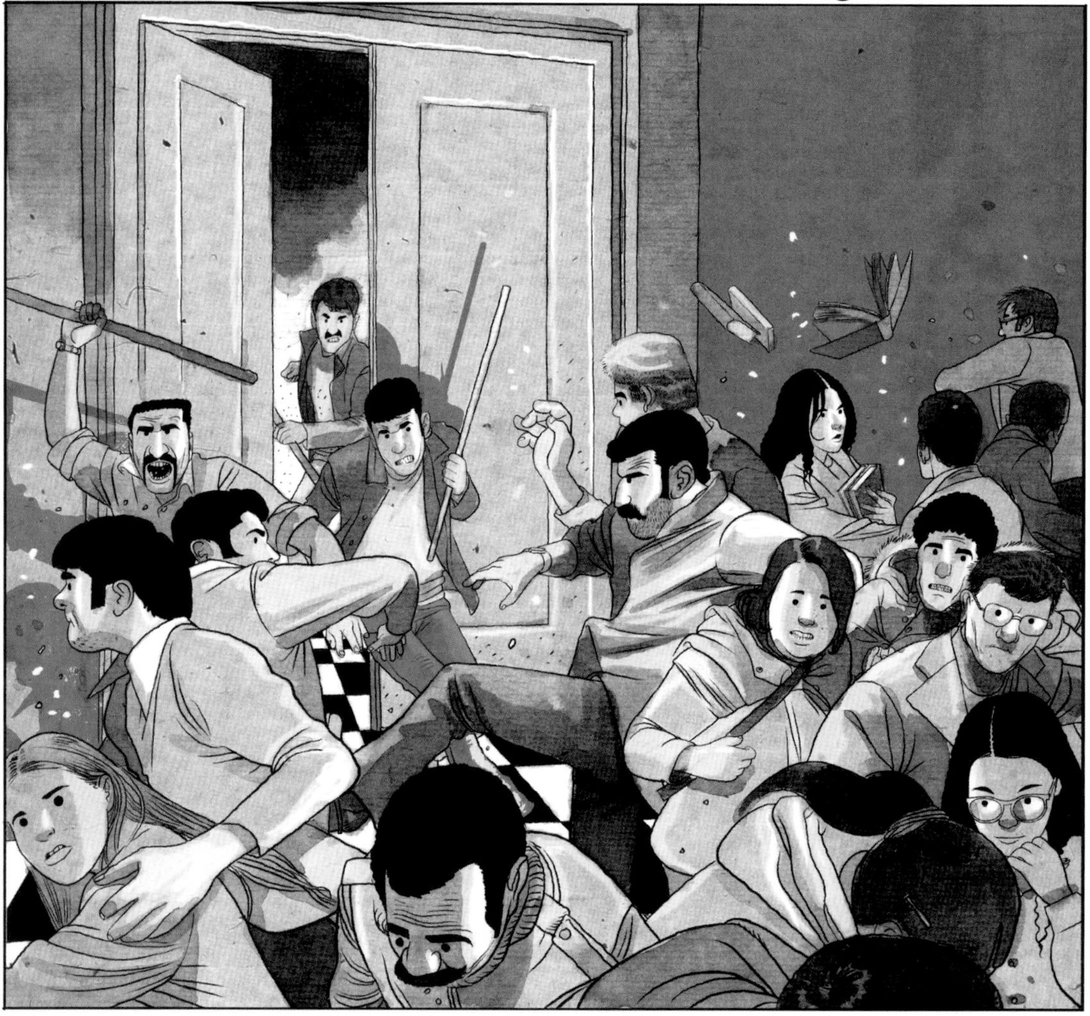

SMACK!
PAHH!

KRAAK

!?

CRACK

FIRST THE LEFTISTS ATE LUNCH.

THEN THE POLICE ESCORTED THE RIGHTISTS INTO THE HALL TO EAT.

GO GUARD THE DOOR.

ER... ALRIGHT.

WHAT ARE YOU DOING WITH THOSE FASCISTS?

I DON'T KNOW.

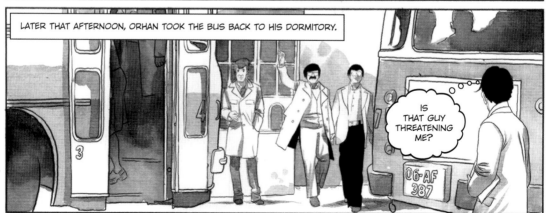

LATER THAT AFTERNOON, ORHAN TOOK THE BUS BACK TO HIS DORMITORY.

IS THAT GUY THREATENING ME?

06-AF 387

24

IN OUR DORMITORY LIVED MANY YOUNG MEN LIKE ME FROM CONSERVATIVE FAMILIES.

ERKEK ÖĞRENCİ YURDU

İSLAM MİRAÇTIR ÜLKÜ SANCAKTIR MUKADDES YOLDAN DÖ...LACAKTIR

THEY WANT TO BURN THE TURKISH NATION TO THE GROUND, ARREST THE NATIONALISTS, AND MAKE OUR HOMELAND A SATELLITE TO ANOTHER COUNTRY!

BROTHER, WHAT TIME ARE YOU LEAVING TOMORROW? CAN I GO WITH YOU?

HAH, FINALLY YOU CHOSE A SIDE. SO YOU'RE JOINING US.

JUST ON THE BUS.

THE NEXT MORNING.

* GRAFFITI: THE MHP FLAG HAS THREE CRESCENT MOONS.   ** GRAFFITI: ISLAM IS HERITAGE, THE NATION IS A BANNER.
*** THE WOLF HAND SIGNAL MADE BY IDEALIST HEARTH AND MHP MEMBERS REFERS TO THE LEGEND OF THE SHE-WOLF THAT LED THE ANCESTORS OF THE TURKS TO SAFETY THROUGH THE MOUNTAINS OF CENTRAL ASIA.

MARTYRS ARE IMMORTAL. OUR LAND IS INDIVISIBLE.

STOP, DON'T BE A FOOL.

\* BANNER: THERE'S NO ROOM AT HACETTEPE FOR FASCISTS.

LOOK, I JUST WANT TO STUDY.

THAT'S WHY I CAME HERE. LET ME THROUGH.

FASCIST.

PLOMFFF!

27

IT'S NOT FAIR. I CAN'T USE ANYTHING AT THE UNIVERSITY, NOT THE GYM, NOT THE CAFE. THEY WON'T LET US IN.

WHERE DID YOU GET THAT?

I USED MY STUDENT LOAN MONEY. IT'S A CZECH-MADE 7.65 MM PISTOL WITH SEVEN BULLETS.

YOU KNOW SOMEONE WHO SELLS...?

VILLAGERS. ALL OF US HAVE A VILLAGE. YOU PAY CASH. THE SAME PEOPLE SELL TO ANYONE, LEFT OR RIGHT.

!

!?

POW!

HACETTEPE DE FAŞİSTLERE YER YOK!

POW!

28

* KAHVEHANE: COFFEEHOUSE

THESE PEOPLE ARE POURING GAS ON OUR COUNTRY AND WE'RE THE FIRE BRIGADE.

WHOK!

!

KriNraKt

THIS IS INSANITY. WHERE ARE THE POLICE? THIS IS THE MAIN ROAD, FOR GOD'S SAKE. WHERE'S THE STATE?

DIRTY COMMUNIST.

YOU GODLESS... ......

Faruk

AT THAT MOMENT, I THOUGHT OF MY FATHER IN ERZURUM, MY BIGGEST HERO. HE TOLD ME I CAME FROM A LINE OF GREAT TURKISH WARRIORS. WE RESISTED THE CRUSADERS, THE RUSSIANS, AND ALL THE OTHER FOREIGN STATES ATTACKING US. EVEN MY MOTHER'S LULLABIES URGED ME TO AVENGE OUR COUNTRY'S VIOLATIONS.

"SLEEP, BABY, SLEEP. BRING THE CRESCENT MOON TO THE MOSQUES."*

* FROM THE POEM "SLEEP BABY" BY ZIYA GÖKALP (1876-1924). THE MHP FLAG HAS THREE CRESCENT MOONS.

AS A BOY, I ATTENDED THE NEIGHBORHOOD ÜGB* WITH MY ELDER BROTHER AND NEIGHBORS.

MARTYRS ARE IMMORTAL, OUR LAND IS INDIVISIBLE!

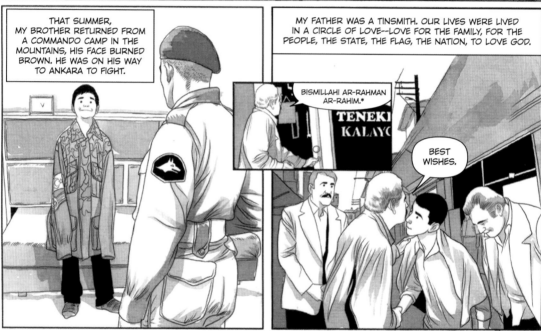

THAT SUMMER, MY BROTHER RETURNED FROM A COMMANDO CAMP IN THE MOUNTAINS, HIS FACE BURNED BROWN. HE WAS ON HIS WAY TO ANKARA TO FIGHT.

MY FATHER WAS A TINSMITH. OUR LIVES WERE LIVED IN A CIRCLE OF LOVE--LOVE FOR THE FAMILY, FOR THE PEOPLE, THE STATE, THE FLAG, THE NATION, TO LOVE GOD.

BISMILLAHI AR-RAHMAN AR-RAHIM.*

BEST WISHES.

THESE WERE MY MORAL GUARDIANS. FROM THE FIRST PRAYER, WE CHILDREN DRANK IN THE PRINCIPLES OF NOBLE BEHAVIOR, GRACE, AND KINDNESS. AT PRAYER TIME, ALL THE MEN LEFT THEIR SHOPS OPEN.

* ÜGB: IDEALIST YOUTH UNION
** BISMILLAH: THE OPENING PHRASE OF THE QURAN

BABA, GIVE ME PERMISSION TO JOIN MY ELDER BROTHER. I WANT TO FIGHT FOR OUR NATION.

BABA, DON'T TALK LIKE THAT. YOU ARE EVERYTHING TO US. BUT I WANT TO BE USEFUL TO MY COUNTRY TOO.

MY DEAR SON, WHAT GOOD IS A HERO IF HIS FAMILY'S HEARTH IS EXTINGUISHED? YOUR DUTY AS A MAN IS TO CONTINUE THE FAMILY LINE AND TO SUPPORT YOUR SISTER AND YOUR MOTHER. I WON'T LIVE FOREVER, YOU KNOW.

IN THAT CASE, GO AND STUDY MEDICINE IN ANKARA. YOU DID WELL ON YOUR EXAMS; YOU HAVE AN OPPORTUNITY. TAKE IT. THEN COME BACK TO SERVE YOUR COMMUNITY AND SUPPORT YOUR FAMILY. YOU HAVE MY BLESSING.

BEFORE I LEFT, WE HAD AN ENGAGEMENT PARTY FOR MY SISTER. MY FATHER ARRANGED FOR HER TO MARRY HIS FRIEND'S SON, WHO LIVED IN GERMANY.

IF ANYTHING HAPPENS TO ME, GOD FORBID, ALL OF MY CHILDREN WILL BE SETTLED IN LIFE.

BUT BEFORE I COULD LEAVE FOR ANKARA, MY BROTHER WAS MARTYRED BY THESE GODLESS COMMUNISTS.

ANKARA: HACETTEPE UNIVERSITY.

RNNNGGG

Orhan

# HONOR

AFTER CLASS.

TUMP!

!?

HEY, THERE WAS A DOOR HERE YESTERDAY.

THERE WAS SHOOTING IN HERE YESTERDAY, SO THEY PUT WALLBOARD UP. WE CALLED THIS CORRIDOR THE PONDEROSA.

WHAT HAPPENED?

THEY ARRESTED SOME OF THE TEACHERS. THEY BROUGHT THEM INTO THE AMPHITHEATER AND ROUGHED THEM UP.

DO YOU KNOW WHO?

!?

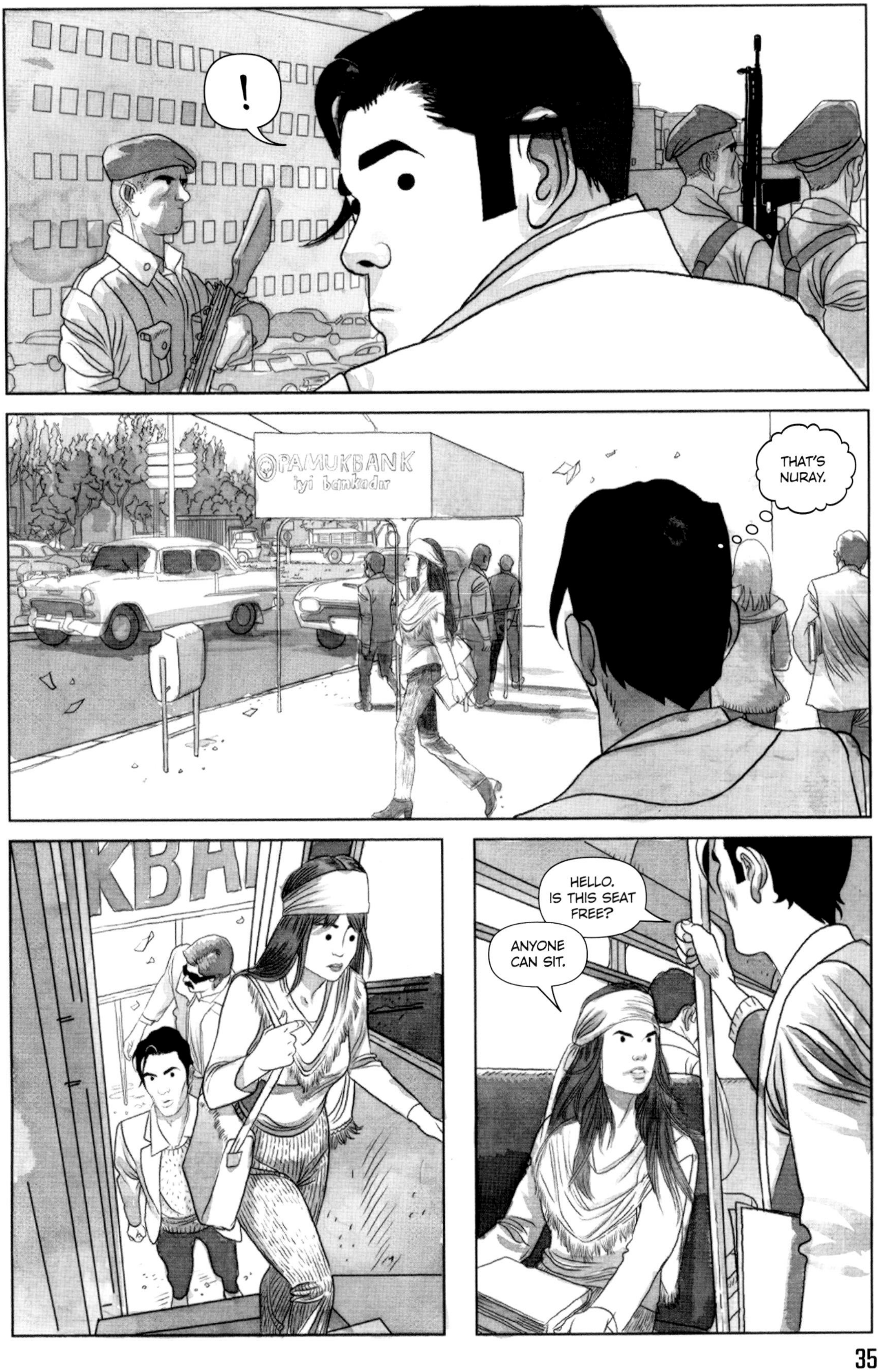
!
PAMUKBANK
iyi bankadır
THAT'S NURAY.
HELLO. IS THIS SEAT FREE?
ANYONE CAN SIT.

THIS STATE IS OURS, WE ARE THE NATION.

!?

THUMP!

AAAHH!

CALM DOWN. YOU'RE SAFE WITH ME.

36

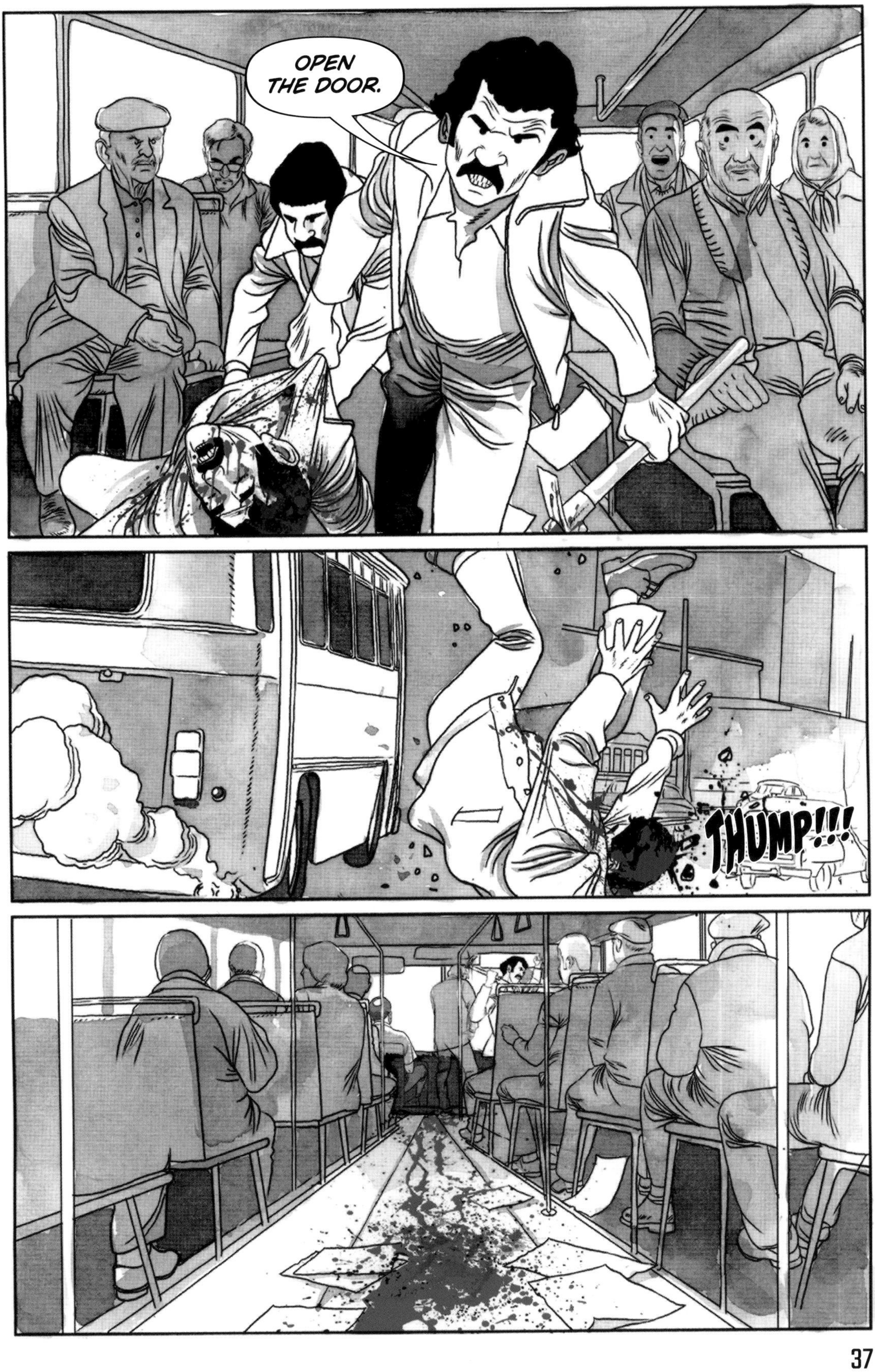
OPEN THE DOOR.
THUMP!!!

* GRAFFITI: LOVE IT OR LEAVE IT. COMMUNISTS TO MOSCOW.

YOU KNOW WHERE I AM. SEE YOU TONIGHT.

I SHOULD LEAVE. I THOUGHT WE WERE ALL GOING TO THE CAFE TOGETHER.

SO DID I. WELL, WHY NOT? SHALL WE DRINK TEA?

IS THAT NURAY?

SHE'S WITH YUNUS!

!

YOU THINK I'M WEAK, BUT I COULD BRING FARUK. IF HE COMES WITH FIFTY PEOPLE, THEY'LL BEAT YOU UP.

BUT NURAY MIGHT GET HURT TOO.

FORGET ABOUT IT. LET HIM SIT WITH HER.

39

MY GOD, WHY DIDN'T HE REACT TO ME? DID HE NOT SEE ME?

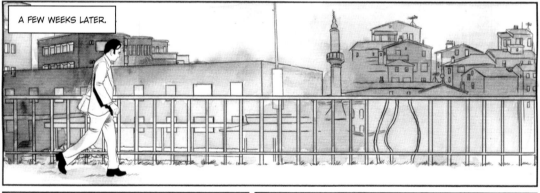

A FEW WEEKS LATER.

YUNUS?!

!

LATER THAT DAY IN A RIGHTIST COFFEEHOUSE.

SÜMBÜL KIRAATHANESi

YOU'RE SUCH A ROMANTIC.

FARUK, HE SAW ME. HE COULD HAVE KILLED ME. BUT HE PAID BACK THE THING I DID IN THE CAFE WHEN I COULD HAVE CALLED YOU, BUT I DIDN'T. I MEAN, AN IDEALIST AND A COMMUNIST, TWO ENEMIES TO THE DEATH. I DID HIM A FAVOR AND HE DID ME A FAVOR. HE HAD A DEBT OF HONOR AND HE PAID IT.

*KIRAATHANE: MEN'S COFFEEHOUSE

## Nuray

# ESKİŞEHİR
### 1973

MY FAMILY LIVED IN A VILLAGE BECAUSE GRANDFATHER NEEDED MY FATHER'S HELP TO FARM THE LAND. MY ELDER BROTHER, FIKRET, AND I WENT TO SCHOOL THERE. MY ELDER SISTER, BILGE, LIVED IN ISTANBUL WITH MY MOTHER'S MOTHER AND ATTENDED UNIVERSITY. GRANDFATHER WAS THE VILLAGE IMAM, BUT, LIKE THE OTHER VILLAGERS, MY FATHER WASN'T SO RELIGIOUS.

AT WEDDINGS, WE DANCED AND SANG, BOYS AND GIRLS TOGETHER. THE MEN DRANK ALCOHOL AND SOMETIMES THERE WAS A BELLY DANCER.

THE VILLAGE TEACHERS WERE ENLIGHTENED NATIONALISTS. THEY TAUGHT ALL THE STUDENTS, EVEN GIRLS, TO GET USED TO READING.

MY PARENTS MOVED TO THE CITY OF ESKİŞEHİR SO I COULD ATTEND SCHOOL THERE. MY FATHER FOUND WORK IN A SUGAR FACTORY. THE REVOLUTIONARY TEACHERS TAUGHT US TURKISH CLASSIC LITERATURE, NOVELS, ADVENTURES, WORLD CLASSICS, STORIES ABOUT PEASANTS OPPRESSED BY LANDLORDS.

I'M BEGINNING TO VISUALIZE A TURKISH SOCIETY.

NAMIK KEMAL

yaşar kemal ince memed

KÖROĞLU

Orhan Veli

CAHİT SITKI TARANCI

OTUZ BEŞ YAŞ

BE MODEST, NURAY. IT'S RAMAZAN AND EVERYONE IS FASTING.

MOM, YOU KNOW I DON'T BELIEVE IN GOD. WHY SHOULD ANYBODY FAST? IT'S OF NO INTEREST TO ME.

SIR, WOULD YOU PLEASE SAY SOMETHING TO YOUR DAUGHTER?

IT'S THOSE FRIENDS OF HERS AT SCHOOL.

LOOK, MY DAUGHTER, DON'T GET INVOLVED. LOOK TO YOUR OWN AFFAIRS.

OF COURSE, FATHER, BUT MAKING THE WORLD A BETTER PLACE, THAT IS MY AFFAIR. WE'RE ALL RESPONSIBLE FOR THAT.

RIGHTIST STUDENTS WAITED FOR LEFTIST STUDENTS TO COME OUT OF THEIR HIGH SCHOOL.

WE HAVE TO HELP OUR ELDER BROTHERS AND SISTERS.

THOOM!

FWEEFEEEE!
FWEEE!

POLIS

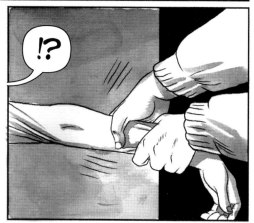

!?

44

WHAT'S YOUR NAME? I'M YUNUS.

NURAY.

WOULD YOU LIKE TO HELP US?

US?

THKP-C*

SURE. WHAT CAN I DO?

A FEW WEEKS LATER AT SCHOOL.

6 FEN B

DO YOU WANT TO JOIN THKP-C. IT'S A MOVEMENT TO CHANGE THE SYSTEM, INSTEAD OF JUST REACTING WEAKLY TO THINGS, LIKE THROWING ROCKS.

WE CAN MAKE A DIFFERENCE!

* THKP-C: PEOPLE'S LIBERATION PARTY FRONT OF TURKEY

NURAY'S SISTER, BILGE, WAS VISITING FROM ISTANBUL.

THANKS FOR THESE! IT'S HARD TO KEEP UP WITH THE LATEST MUSIC AND BOOKS HERE IN THE PROVINCES.

NURAY, MOTHER TELLS ME YOU'VE BECOME INVOLVED WITH THKP-C. SHE FOUND LEAFLETS IN YOUR ROOM.

OH. THEY'RE NOT MINE. I'M JUST KEEPING THEM FOR A FRIEND.

YOU DON'T HAVE TO LIE TO ME. I'M GLAD YOU'RE INVOLVED. YOU JUST NEED TO BE MORE CAREFUL. I'M A MEMBER OF TDK*. DON'T TELL ANYONE HERE.

WE HAD NO TELEPHONE. WHEN SHE WAS HERE, SHE USED THE PHONE BOOTH ON THE STREET, ALWAYS LOOKING LEFT AND RIGHT. DOES ANYONE SEE HER? IS ANYONE FOLLOWING HER?

* TDK: REVOLUTIONARY WOMEN'S UNION OF TURKEY

THE POLICE RAIDED OUR ORGANIZATION LAST WEEK. IT'S LUCKY THAT I WASN'T CAUGHT. THEY FOUND MY NAME. THE POLICE PICKED UP MY FRIEND GÜL AND ASKED FOR MY ADDRESS, BUT I HAD JUST MOVED, SO GÜL DIDN'T KNOW IT.

SHE'S THE ONE WHO BELONGS TO A UNION. SHE LEFT THE UNIVERSITY TO WORK IN A TEXTILE FACTORY SO SHE COULD MOBILIZE THE WORKERS.

I WANT TO BE LIKE THAT.

I SHOULD TELL YOU TO STAY SAFE AND MIND YOUR OWN BUSINESS, BUT I KNOW YOU WON'T LISTEN.

BE VERY CAREFUL, NURAY. DON'T PARTICIPATE IN RAIDS, ESPECIALLY AT NIGHT.

# A SPELL ON THE NATION

25 DECEMBER, 1973

OUR GREAT LEADER IS GONE.

NOW THOSE BIGOTS WILL SEIZE THEIR CHANCE.

* HEADLINE: "İSMET İNÖNÜ DIED ON DECEMBER 25, 1973." İNÖNÜ WAS THE SECOND PRESIDENT OF THE TURKISH REPUBLIC AND SERVED THREE TERMS AS PRIME MINISTER. HE WAS REVERED AS A SECULAR LEADER.

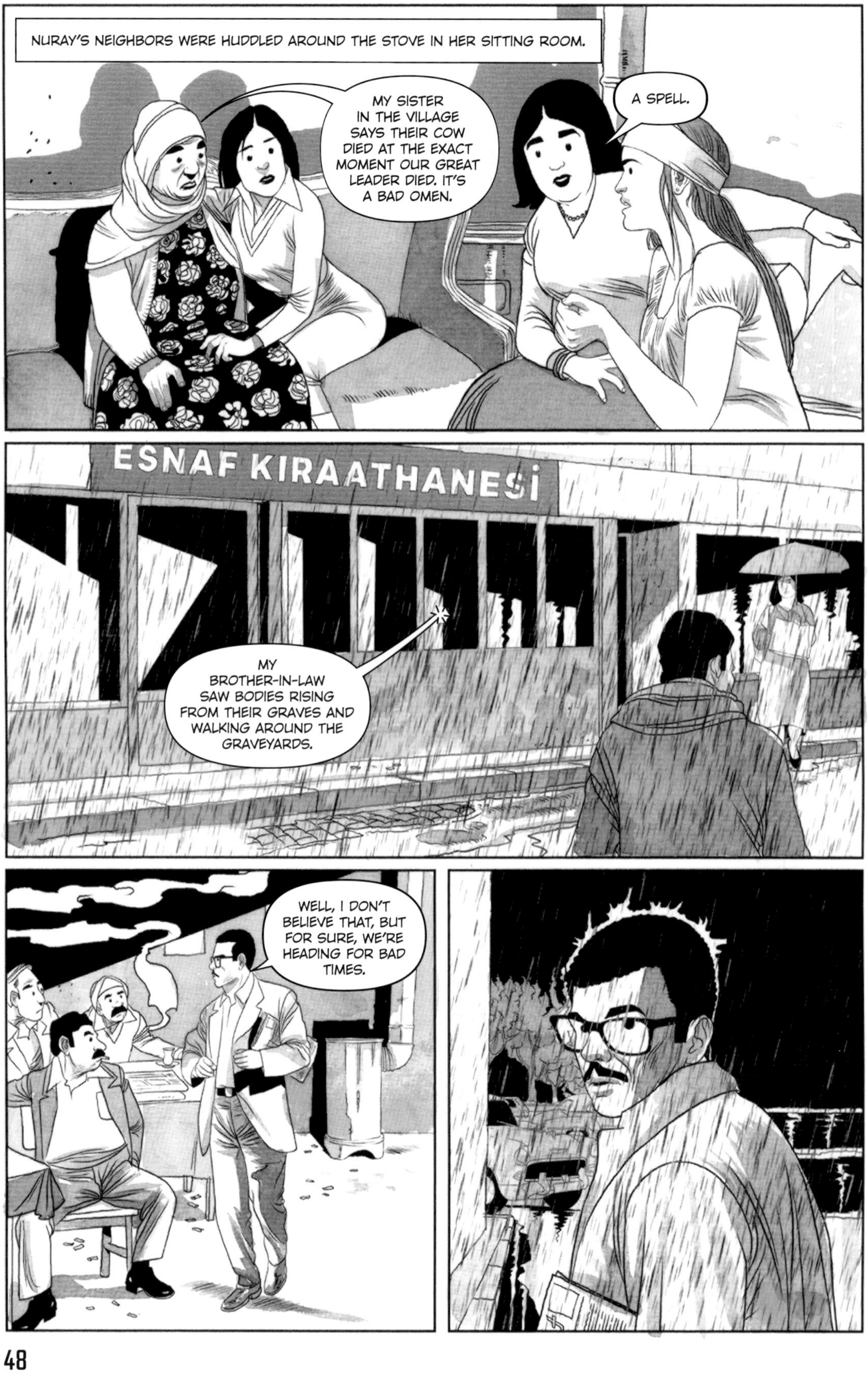
NURAY'S NEIGHBORS WERE HUDDLED AROUND THE STOVE IN HER SITTING ROOM.
MY SISTER IN THE VILLAGE SAYS THEIR COW DIED AT THE EXACT MOMENT OUR GREAT LEADER DIED. IT'S A BAD OMEN.
A SPELL.
ESNAF KIRAATHANESİ
MY BROTHER-IN-LAW SAW BODIES RISING FROM THEIR GRAVES AND WALKING AROUND THE GRAVEYARDS.
WELL, I DON'T BELIEVE THAT, BUT FOR SURE, WE'RE HEADING FOR BAD TIMES.

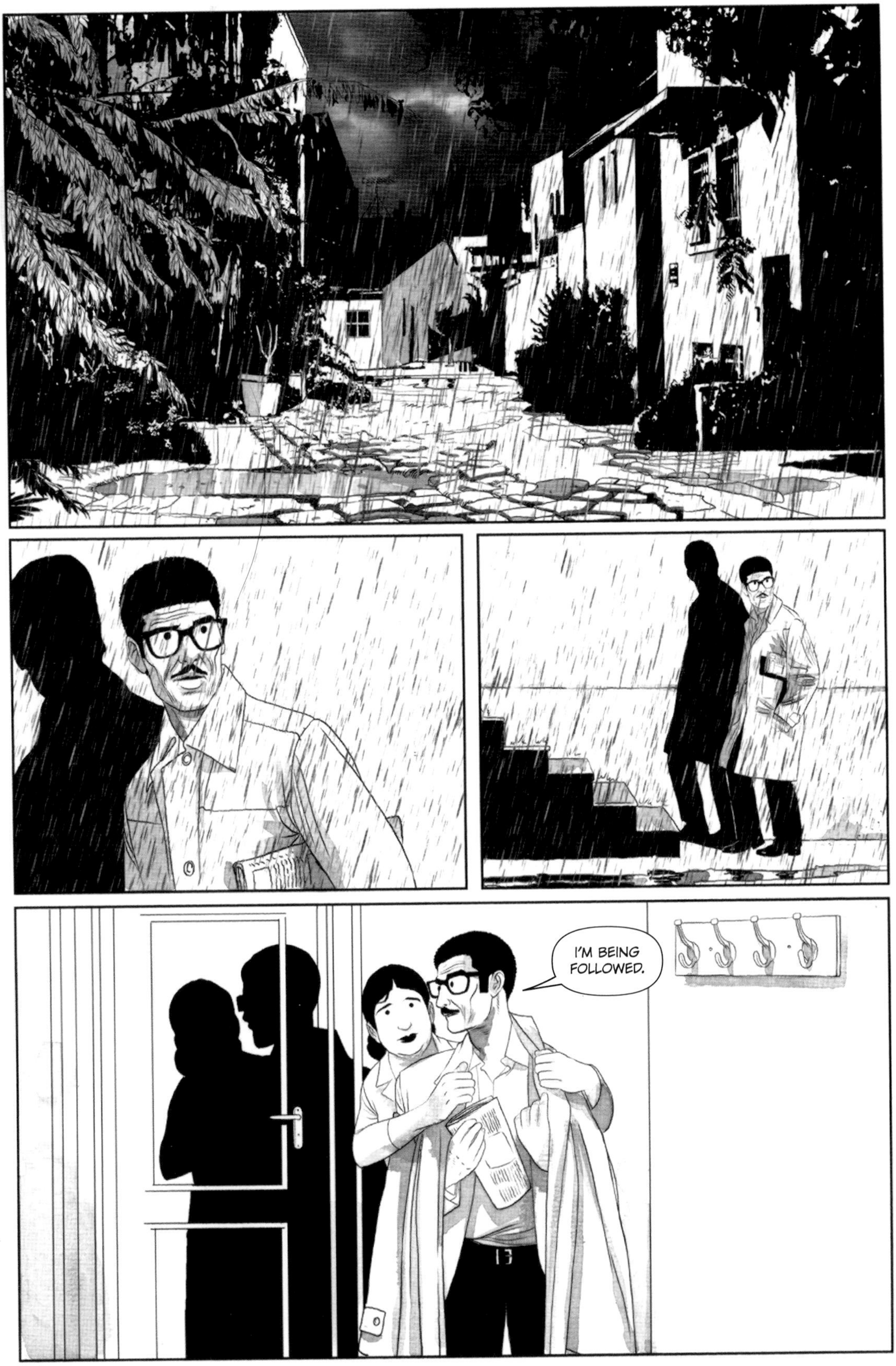
I'M BEING FOLLOWED.

## Yunus

# ESKİŞEHİR
### 1973

IN THE SUMMER, I HELPED PICK CHERRIES ON A NEIGHBOR'S FARM. THEY PAID ME WITH CHEESE FROM THEIR COWS.

MAY IT BRING YOU BLESSINGS, SON.

THANK YOU, AUNTIE.

I SOLD THE CHEESE IN THE MARKET.

THERE I MADE SOME FRIENDS: MEMO, MEATBALL TAHIR, AND BLIND AHMET, WHO WASN'T BLIND. HE HAD A SHOP.

LOOK, MY BOY, THIS IS HOW YOU GRILL MEATBALLS.

WE SAT UNDER A TENT EATING MEATBALLS UNTIL LATE IN THE EVENING.

COME ON, LET'S VISIT TUFAN, A FRIEND OF MINE FROM PRISON.

WE WENT TO A MARKET THAT WAS OPEN LATE.

HI TUFAN. IT'S NOT TOO LATE, IS IT?

NOT AT ALL! YOU'RE VERY WELCOME.

TOWARD DAWN.

MEMO KILLED A MAN AND WENT TO JAIL. TAHIR WORKED AS A WAITER, SLEEPING IN A STABLE. TUFAN FELL IN LOVE WITH A WOMAN AND RAN AWAY WITH HER TO ANKARA, LEAVING HIS WIFE AND CHILDREN. SLOWLY I LOST TOUCH WITH THEM.

I DIDN'T BECOME A MARXIST AS A LIFELONG COMMITMENT. I SIMPLY READ IT AND FOUND IT TRUE.

WHEN I BECAME A MARXIST NO SUCH RELATIONS WITH PEOPLE LIKE TAHIR, MEMO, AND TUFAN REMAINED BECAUSE THEY HAD BECOME "THE PROLETARIAT." THEY HAD NO FACE.

WE VISITED THE HOMES OF SOME FACTORY WORKERS. IT WAS LIKE SOMETHING OUT OF GEORGE ORWELL. THE SMELL WAS BAD.

THEIR RELATIONSHIP WITH US WAS AN ARTIFICIAL, CALCULATED THING.

THERE WAS LITTLE COMMUNICATION WITH THE FOLK. WE DIDN'T KNOW THEM OR SPEAK THEIR LANGUAGE.

WE HAD OTHER CONCERNS.

Summer, 1975
Ankara

# YUNUS AND THE PROLETARIAT

UNTIL UNIVERSITY BEGAN IN THE FALL, YUNUS LIVED WITH HIS GREAT-AUNT SEDEF.

I SPENT THREE YEARS IN MARSEILLES WORKING IN A FACTORY, BUT NOW I HAVE MY OWN BUSINESS HERE. WHAT ARE YOU PLANNING TO DO AFTER UNIVERSITY? MAYBE I CAN MAKE A CONNECTION FOR YOU IN FRANCE.

CAPITALISM IS THE PROBLEM, UNCLE. THE FASCISTS ARE HAND IN HAND WITH THE CAPITALISTS AND THE AMERICANS. WE FIRST NEED TO THROW OFF THE IMPERIALISM THAT'S OPPRESSING OUR PEOPLE.

YOU SHOULD READ THESE.

THE FRENCH WORKING CLASS ISN'T THE SAME AS THE SOVIET PROLETARIAT. A DICTATORSHIP OF THE PROLETARIAT WON'T WORK IN EUROPE. WE AREN'T SOVIETS, ALWAYS FIGHTING EACH OTHER.

WHAT DO YOU MEAN?

PEOPLE LIKE ME WENT TO EUROPE AS WORKERS AND RETURNED WITH MONEY. WE INVESTED IT IN STARTING A BUSINESS, A GROCERY STORE. THERE'S NO SUCH THING AS A PROLETARIAT WITHOUT DREAMS OF PROGRESS. NOBODY WANTS TO STAY A WORKER.

BUT WORKERS ARE STILL OPPRESSED.

THAT'S WHAT UNIONS ARE FOR. READ THE BOOKS.

PAPAZIN BAĞI, ANKARA, FALL 1975

WHEN I ENTERED UNIVERSITY, I MADE NEW FRIENDS.

WE DON'T HAVE A PROPER PROLETARIAT IN TURKEY. THERE AREN'T THAT MANY FACTORIES.

THE WORKERS I KNEW ALL MOVED UP. THEN THEY WEREN'T WORKERS ANYMORE. THEY OWNED MORE PROPERTY.

MEHMET, BRING ME CIGARETTES.

WHAT ABOUT THE HUGE DISK* PROTEST IN 1970? TENS OF THOUSANDS OF WORKERS WALKED OUT OF THE FACTORIES.

DISK

* DISK: REVOLUTIONARY WORKERS' TRADE UNIONS CONFEDERATION. THEY HELD A LARGE PROTEST ON JUNE 15-16, 1970.

THAT ISN'T A PROLETARIAT. THEY'RE MEMBERS OF A UNION. THEY WANT BETTER WAGES, NOT A REVOLUTION.

THAT'S RIGHT. WE'RE AN UNDERDEVELOPED COUNTRY, SO IT'S THE MIDDLE CLASSES THAT ARE IMPORTANT, THE MILITARY OFFICERS, PEOPLE AT THE UNIVERSITY, LIKE US.

YOUR CIGARETTES, SIR.

RASIM, DO YOU HAVE TIME TO GIVE ME A SHINE?

HOW ARE YOU? HOW IS YOUR FAMILY?

THEY'RE DOING WELL, SIR, THANKS TO GENTLEMEN LIKE YOU.

I WAS BOTHERED BY THE HIGH RESPECT RASIM AND MEHMET THE TEA BOY HAD FOR US. MY MARXIST FRIENDS AND I TALKED ABOUT EQUAL OWNERSHIP OF PROPERTY, BUT THERE WAS SOMETHING WRONG. WE READ AND CRITICIZED AS IF WE WERE LIVING IN EUROPE.

THERE'S A SAYING: IN TURKEY, EVEN GOOD THINGS HAVE A BAD OUTCOME. AFTER THE DISK PROTEST, MARTIAL LAW WAS DECLARED ON JUNE 16, 1970, AND EVERYONE INVOLVED WAS ARRESTED.

ANOTHER DAY.

THAT'S WHEN THE VIOLENCE REALLY STARTED, THE LEFT GROUPS COMPETING WITH EACH OTHER.

AND THE BANK ROBBERIES.

TERROR BECAME A KIND OF INDUSTRY.

BANKASI

A YEAR LATER, ON MARCH 12, 1971, THERE WAS A COUP.

THKP* AND DEV-GENC** MEMBERS WERE ARRESTED.

* THKP: PEOPLE'S LIBERATION PARTY OF TURKEY
** DEV-GENÇ: REVOLUTIONARY YOUTH FEDERATION OF TURKEY

## CONGREGATION

SEPTEMBER 1975. YUNUS BEGAN HIS STUDIES AT HACETTEPE UNIVERSITY. HE LIVED IN A LEFTIST DORMITORY.

LET'S GO.

Paris
France

YILMAZ GÜNEY

THE FEELING OF CONGREGATION IS VERY POWERFUL. YOU DO EVERYTHING TOGETHER. YOU ROOT FOR YOUR GUY, ALWAYS CLAP AT WHAT HE SAYS. YOU SUPPORT HIM, EVEN IF YOU DON'T LIKE HIM.

YUNUS ATTENDED AN IGD* MEETING. AN OLDER STUDENT, MUSTAFA, WAS THE GROUP LEADER.

BROTHER MUSTAFA, YOU'RE TALKING ABOUT DICTATORSHIP OF THE PROLETARIAT, BUT IN FRANCE, THEY'RE DISCUSSING ADVANCED DEMOCRACY, HOW THE VIEWS OF ALL THE PEOPLE, NOT JUST THE PROLETARIAT, CAN BECOME POLICY. WE DON'T HAVE A PROLETARIAT IN TURKEY, SO WE NEED A NEW WAY. I BROUGHT SOME ARTICLES AND BOOKS WITH ME.

HOW NICE, GIVE THEM TO ME SO I CAN READ THEM.

GENÇLER D

I'LL WANT THEM BACK.

* IGD: PROGRESSIVE YOUTH ASSOCIATION

LATER THAT EVENING.

THE FASCISTS ARE GOING TO ATTACK THE UNIVERSITY BUSES AT 7 IN THE MORNING. BE THERE!

07:00

THE FASCISTS DIDN'T COME.

THAT AFTERNOON.

LONG LIVE SOCIALISM.

KIRAATHANE

LONG LIVE SOCIALISM.

59

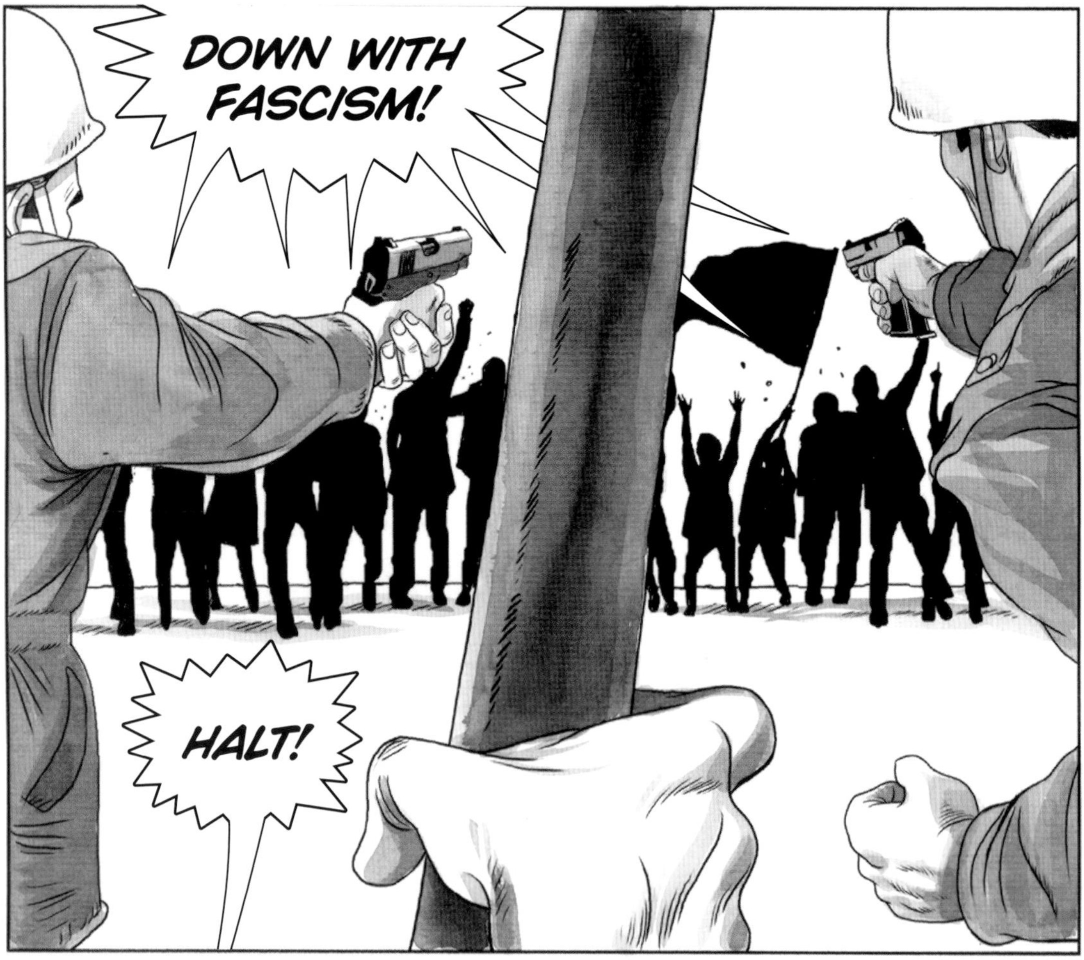
DOWN WITH FASCISM!
HALT!

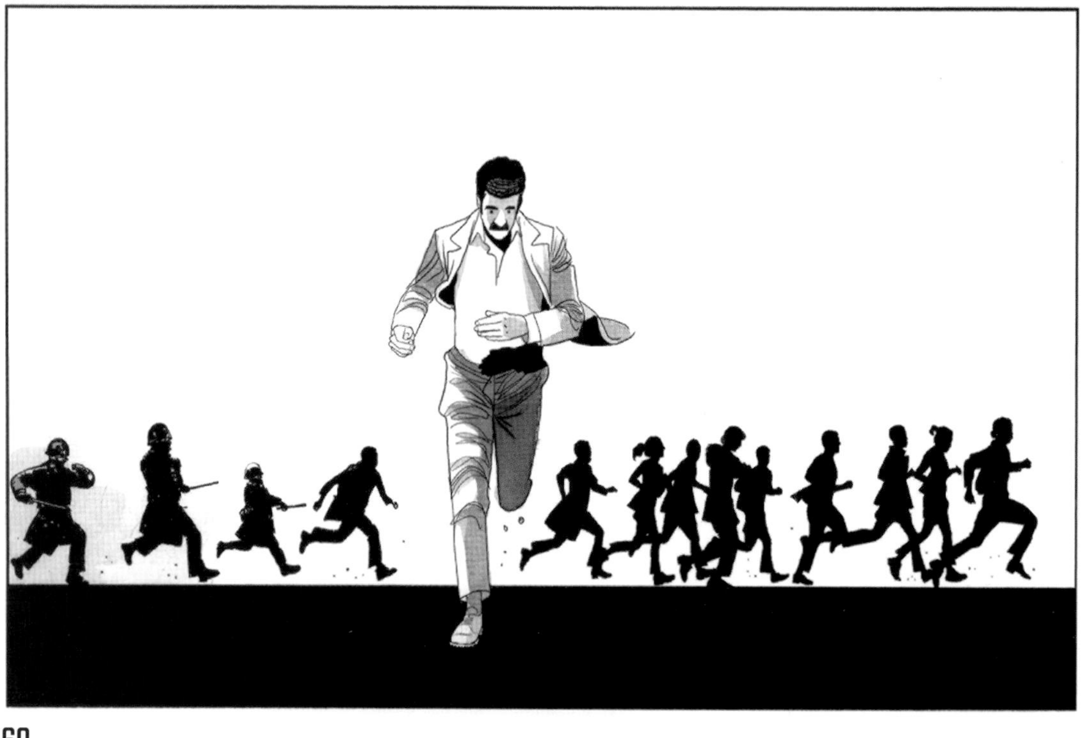

## Feride

# THE BAZAAR

NURAY AND HER FRIEND FERIDE STUDIED MEDICINE AT HACETTEPE UNIVERSITY IN ANKARA. THEY LIVED IN A WOMEN'S DORMITORY.

I'D LIKE TO JOIN A SOCIALIST GROUP, BUT I DON'T KNOW WHICH ONE. IF THEY'RE ALL LEFTIST, HOW CAN THERE BE SO MANY GROUPS?

EVEN THE ONES WITH THE SAME ROOTS FIGHT EACH OTHER. OVER THINGS LIKE WHAT DOES THIS WORD BY MAO MEAN OR THIS SENTENCE BY MARX. YESTERDAY I HEARD THKP-C* AND THKP** STUDENTS ARGUING OVER WHETHER KEMALISM IS A BOURGEOIS IDEOLOGY AND THEREFORE THEY SHOULD REJECT IT, OR WHETHER THEY SHOULD KEEP IT. WHEN THEY STARTED SHOVING EACH OTHER, I LEFT. EVERYBODY WANTS THEIR VERSION OF HISTORY TO BE SUPREME.

CAMPUS IS LIKE A BAZAAR, EVERY GROUP TRYING TO SELL ITSELF. YOU CAN'T JOIN EVERYTHING.

WHAT DID YOU DECIDE IN THE END?

WELL, I JOINED THE IKD*** BECAUSE THEY WERE MY FRIENDS. I'M ALSO IN THKP-C. A FRIEND FROM ESKIŞEHIR BELONGS TO IT. BUT I'M NOT SURE I'LL STAY.

WHY NOT?

THEY HOLD MEETING AFTER MEETING IN SMALL ROOMS, EVERYONE SMOKES AND ARGUES. I'M ALWAYS WORRIED THAT THE FASCISTS WILL BREAK IN OR THE POLICE. MY BROTHER SAID IF I GET A POLICE RECORD, I CAN'T BE A DOCTOR. IN THE IKD, I JUST DO RESEARCH AND PREPARE BROCHURES.

I KNOW WHAT YOU MEAN. I'VE STAYED AWAY FROM THE DEMONSTRATIONS.

BUT IT'S IMPOSSIBLE TO AVOID. ON THE UNIVERSITY BUS THE OTHER DAY, THE FASCISTS HIT A GUY ON THE HEAD WITH A HAMMER AND PUSHED HIM OUT ONTO THE ROAD. I DIDN'T SEE ANYTHING IN THE NEWSPAPERS ABOUT IT, SO MAYBE HE DIDN'T DIE.

HOW AWFUL. I DON'T THINK THEY PRINT STUFF LIKE THAT. IT'S TOO COMMON.

WHEN THEY KILL OUR PROFESSORS, THAT GETS IN THE NEWS.

SOMEONE I KNEW FROM CLASS WAS ON THAT BUS. I THOUGHT HE WAS A NICE GUY, BUT I GUESS YOU CAN NEVER KNOW.

* THKP-C: PEOPLE'S LIBERATION PARTY/FRONT OF TURKEY
** THKP: PEOPLE'S LIBERATION PARTY OF TURKEY
*** IKD: PROGRESSIVE WOMEN'S ASSOCIATION

TELL ME ABOUT WHERE YOU GREW UP.

WHEN I WAS YOUNG, ADANA WAS A SMALL PLACE WHERE EVERYONE KNEW EACH OTHER. IT WAS AN AGRICULTURAL CITY. THERE WAS ALMOST NO TRAFFIC. LIFE WAS INEXPENSIVE, LOTS OF FRUITS AND VEGETABLES. I WENT TO GRADE SCHOOL NEAR MY HOUSE.

SOME CHILDREN WERE POOR, OTHERS WEALTHY. SOME CAME TO SCHOOL IN SLIPPERS. THE PRINCIPAL COLLECTED MONEY AND BOUGHT THEM NOTEBOOKS, BOOKS, SCHOOLBAGS, AND CLOTHES.

WHERE DID YOU GET THOSE NICE COLORED PENCILS?

MY COUSIN BROUGHT THEM FROM GERMANY.

THE UNITED STATES MILITARY BASE WAS NEARBY. OUR NEXT-DOOR NEIGHBORS WERE A MILITARY FAMILY. I LEARNED A FEW WORDS OF ENGLISH. THEY GAVE US BIG, DECORATED CHOCOLATE CAKES AND MAGAZINES.

COME ON OVER, FRIEDA! HAVE SOME CAKE.

COMING, MRS. CALLAHAN.

TRY SOME TURKISH FOOD!

WE DIDN'T HAVE A TELEVISION. WHEN I WAS IN HIGH SCHOOL, MY FATHER BOUGHT A SMALL GRUNDIG RADIO WITH AN ANTENNA. IT MADE ME WANT TO LEARN ENGLISH.

SHUT OFF THAT RADIO! I'M STUDYING.

THERE WERE ALSO MARCHES AND POLICE. I HEARD THAT THEY KILLED JOURNALISTS, A SCHOOL PRINCIPAL, AND A BANKER. I USUALLY ATE LUNCH AT HOME.

ONE DAY, AS I WAS WALKING BACK TO SCHOOL AFTER LUNCH, A GROUP APPROACHED.

A SECOND GROUP CAME FROM THE OTHER SIDE.

THE POLICE CAME AND ARRESTED THEM.

THE SAME THING HAPPENED IN ESKİŞEHİR.

THE GROCERY STORE IN OUR BUILDING WAS CLOSED BECAUSE ITS OWNER WAS MHP. A LEFTIST KILLED HIM.

BOOM!

THEY OPENED A NEW TURKISH AIRLINES OFFICE IN OUR BUILDING. TEN DAYS LATER A BOMB BROKE ALL THE WINDOWS.

THEN THEY SHOT UP THE BILLIARD SALON. EVERYONE SPECULATED ABOUT WHO DID IT.

BİLARDO SALONU

HOW AWFUL. SOME OF OUR YOUNG RELATIVES GOT INVOLVED. ONE OF MY COUSINS TOOK HOSTAGES ON CAMPUS. HE ESCAPED AND LEFT TOWN. THE POLICE ARE LOOKING FOR HIM.

IN MY FAMILY, WE DEBATED POLITICS OPENLY. MY FATHER SUPPORTED THE JUSTICE PARTY. MY MOTHER WAS FOR THE REPUBLICAN PEOPLE'S PARTY. THEY READ DIFFERENT NEWSPAPERS. THERE WERE NO ARGUMENTS.

IF FAMILIES FIGHT, CHILDREN FIGHT. YOU CAN'T SAVE YOURSELF. I ALWAYS WONDERED WHICH SIDE I WAS ON.

I LEFT SCHOOL BECAUSE OF THE VIOLENCE. WE MOVED TO ANKARA SO I COULD FINISH, BUT WE COULDN'T ESCAPE IT. WE WERE MAKING PASTA. I LOOKED OUT THE WINDOW AND SAW SOME MEN GRAB A GUY AND SHOOT HIM.

THEY WORE ORANGE SWEATERS THAT THEY PULLED OFF AND THREW AWAY, SO THE EYE WAS FOOLED AND THEY COULDN'T BE FOLLOWED.

IT HAPPENED SEVEN TIMES. AT THE FIRST ONE, YOU SAY, OH MY GOD. YOUR STOMACH HEAVES, YOU CAN'T EAT. BY THREE OR FOUR YOU GET USED TO IT.

WHO DID IT?

ONE DAY THE POLICE SET A TRAP ON OUR STREET. THEY SHOT THEM IN THE LEGS. WHEN THEY FELL, THE POLICE CAUGHT THEM.

WE DON'T KNOW WHO DID IT. COULD HAVE BEEN MAFIA.

I HAD A NEIGHBOR, YUSUF. HE WAS MARRIED, WITH CHILDREN. HE WAS NEITHER LEFT NOR RIGHT, NOT THE TYPE TO GET INVOLVED IN THINGS LIKE THIS. ONE DAY, AN OLD FRIEND WHO HAD JOINED MHP CAME TO HIM.

YUSUF BROTHER, TODAY DON'T GO OUT THE FRONT DOOR OF THE BUILDING, GO OUT THE BACK.

MY GOD, WHAT'S GOING ON?

THE RIGHTISTS STRAFED THE FRONT OF THE HOUSE WITH BULLETS AND KILLED SEVEN PEOPLE.

YUSUF CRIED FOR DAYS.

WHY DID I LEAVE AND NOT WARN EVERYONE NOT TO GO OUT THE FRONT?

AND NOW IT'S HERE. I WISH I KNEW WHAT IT WAS ALL FOR.

! !

BANG!

## Yunus

# THE REVOLUTION IS FULL TIME

* DAZ: REVOLUTIONARY MORALITY POLICE

MY GOD, THEY'RE LEFTISTS. *RUN.*

I'M WITH IGD.*

SO, THAT DOESN'T MEAN WE SHOULD LET YOU GO AROUND RAPING OUR VALUES.

THERE WASN'T ANY JOY REALLY, THOUGH THERE WAS TALK OF BRIGHT HORIZONS, OF THE GLORIOUS FUTURE, SOCIALISM. BUT IT WASN'T A SMILING THING.

MIDNIGHT

WHY DO WE HAVE TO KEEP WATCH EVERY NIGHT. IT'S AS IF WE'RE SOLDIERS. NOTHING'S GOING TO HAPPEN.

THE POLICE CAN RAID US, THE FASCISTS CAN RAID US. REVOLUTION IS FULL TIME, NOT JUST DURING THE DAY.

* IGD: PROGRESSIVE YOUTH ASSOCIATION

LOOK! WHAT'S THAT?

IT'S THE CYPRIOT TURKISH IGD. THEIR MEMBERS RAN AWAY FROM CYPRIOT TURKISH DEV-YOL* AND FORMED A NEW GROUP.

LET US IN, LET US IN. DEV-YOL IS ATTACKING. WILL YOU PROTECT US?

LET'S GO UPSTAIRS.

DON'T LET THEM IN!

OPEN THE DOOR!

GROUPS SPLIT OVER THE SMALLEST THINGS INTO FACTIONS THAT THEN DESPISED AND FOUGHT EACH OTHER. THEY KNEW ALL MY SECRETS, MY PRIVATE LIFE, THEY KNEW EVERYTHING ABOUT ME.

THEN SUDDENLY THEY SEPARATED AND, IN THAT MOMENT, THEY BECAME MY GREATEST ENEMY.

* DEV-YOL: REVOLUTIONARY PATH

69

STOP. WE WANT TO NEGOTIATE.

WE ARE GOING TO MOVE AWAY BUT YOU MUST LEAVE YOUR WEAPONS. ALL OF YOU TRAITORS HAVE TO LEAVE THE BUILDING.

WILL WE HAVE SAFE CONDUCT?

YES. I GIVE MY WORD AS A REVOLUTIONARY.

WHAT RAGE, WHAT HATRED! I MEAN THIS WASN'T JUST ABOUT A SIMPLE POLITICAL DIFFERENCE, THERE WAS SOMETHING INCREDIBLE ABOUT SUCH ENMITY. WHAT COULD CONTINUALLY REPRODUCE SUCH A SICKNESS?

HELLO, BROTHER MUSTAFA.

HOW DARE YOU. YOU'VE BEEN TALKING ABOUT ME TO EVERYBODY, TELLING THEM I DON'T GIVE BOOKS BACK.

WELL, YOU DIDN'T GIVE THEM BACK.

I DECIDE WHAT YOU READ.

HOW CAN THIS BE? YOU'RE TALKING ABOUT SOCIALISM, EQUALITY AND STUFF. IS THIS WHAT IT MEANS TO BE A LEADER?

# BATTLE OF THE POSTERS

THEN I GOT SHOT. ONE OF THOSE BULLETS IS STILL IN ME.

\* POSTERS: SGB, SOCIALIST YOUTH UNION

THE NEXT MORNING.

LOOK AT THAT! HOW DARE THEY HANG THEIR POSTERS OVER OUR POSTERS.

THAT EVENING.

BREAK DOWN THE DOOR AND SMASH EVERYTHING.

THEY WON'T DISHONOR US AGAIN.

SEVGI, CAN YOU HELP ME HANG THIS? I'M SO TIRED.

OF COURSE, NURAY. THESE POSTERS ARE READY. AND I'M READY TO GO HOME!

I DON'T LIKE BEING HERE ALONE. WHAT'S THAT SOUND?

ALLAH, ALLAH.

BAMM

RUN, TELL THE GUYS.

* İGD: PROGRESSIVE YOUTH ASSOCIATION

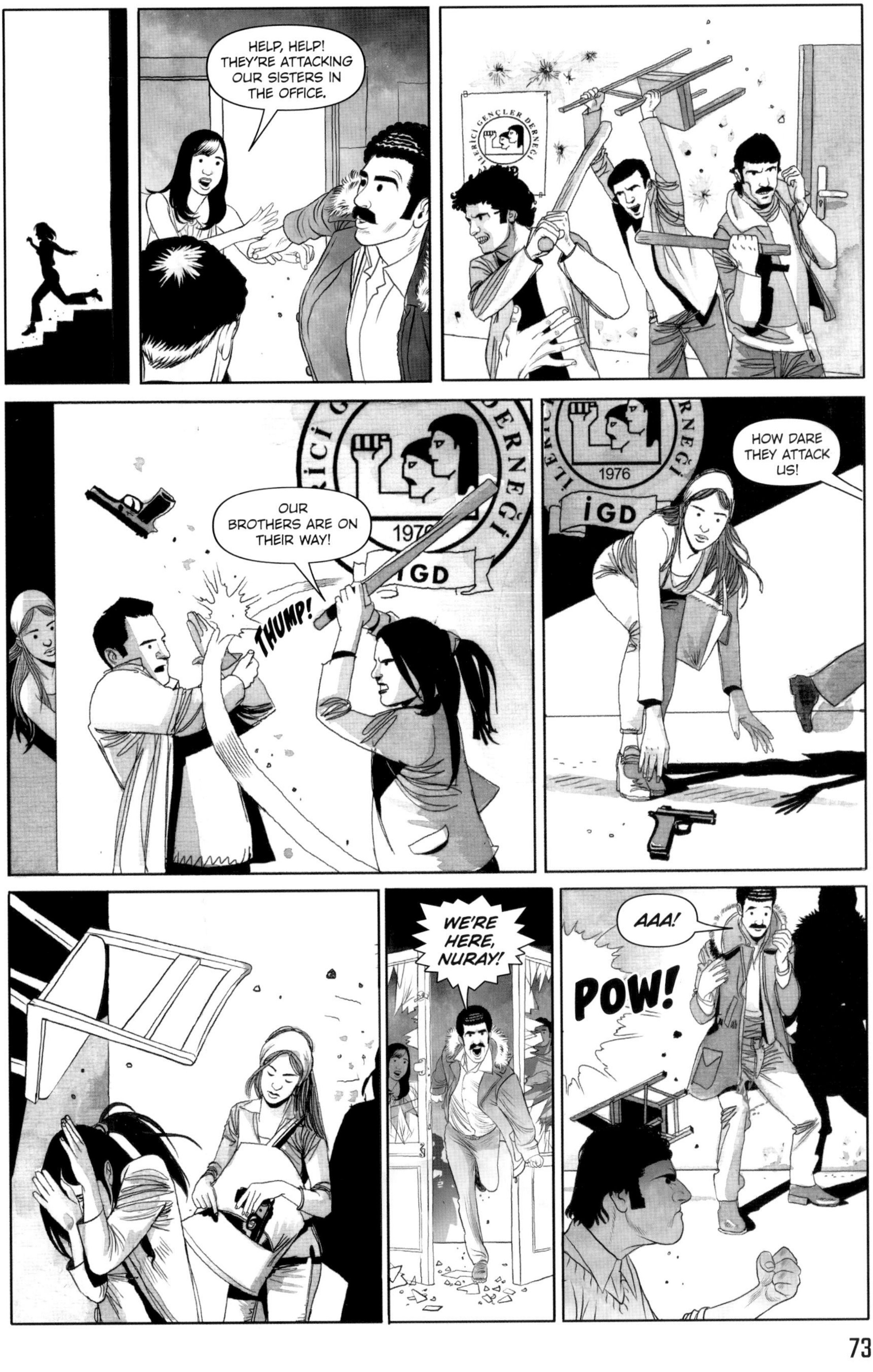
HELP, HELP! THEY'RE ATTACKING OUR SISTERS IN THE OFFICE.
İLERİCİ GENÇLER DERNEĞİ
OUR BROTHERS ARE ON THEIR WAY!
THUMP!
1976
İGD
HOW DARE THEY ATTACK US!
WE'RE HERE, NURAY!
AAA!
POW!

HOW DARE YOU SHOOT AT US.

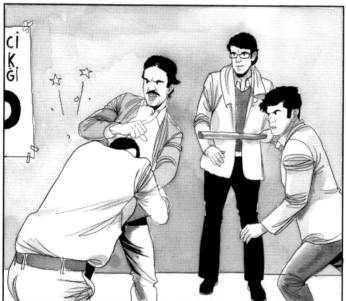

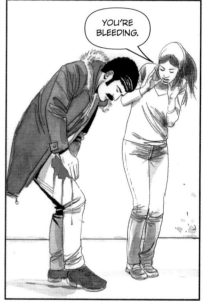

YOU'RE BLEEDING.

THAT NIGHT AT THE POLICE STATION.

T.C. POLİS KARAKOLU

WHO ATTACKED YOU?

WE DON'T KNOW THEM.

WHY DIDN'T YOU PRESS CHARGES? THEY SHOT YOU!

WE CAN'T COMPLAIN ABOUT A LEFTIST TO THE POLICE; IT'S NOT DONE. IT WOULD BE SHAMEFUL, AS IF WE WERE THE POLICE.

I WAS THE ONLY ONE WHO GOT SHOT ANYWAY.

WHAT ABOUT THE TRIALS? PEOPLE CLAIM THERE ARE POLICE SPIES AND THEN THERE'S A TRIAL. NOT EVEN A PROPER TRIAL, JUST SOME KIDS IN A CLASSROOM. THEY TELL THE KIDS THEY'RE GUILTY OF BETRAYING US AND THEN THEY'RE TAKEN SOMEWHERE AND BEATEN UP OR EXECUTED. AREN'T WE ACTING JUST LIKE THE POLICE?

I AGREE, IT'S WRONG. IT DAMAGES OUR REVOLUTIONARY STRUGGLE TO COLD-BLOODEDLY ORDER SOMEONE EXECUTED. IT'S NOT LIKE FIGHTING OUT OF ANGER.

ARE YOU IN PAIN?

THREE BULLETS. THE BULLET I GOT IN MY HIP COULD ACTUALLY HAVE GONE HERE. I COULD HAVE BEEN PARALYZED. I COULD BE DEAD.

YUNUS WENT TO SEE MUSTAFA, THE HEAD OF HIS IGD GROUP.

MUSTAFA, I WANT TO REST. FOR A TIME, I WON'T BE GOING OUT HANGING POSTERS, I WON'T BE GOING TO THE PROTESTS. LEAVE ME ALONE FOR A WHILE.

75

SO, ARE WE GOING TO SAY NOW THAT YUNUS WENT ON HOLIDAY? WHILE THE MOVEMENT STRUGGLE GOES ON, WE CAN'T SAY THAT YUNUS WANTS TO REST. WE CAN'T DO THAT.

WELL, THAT'S UP TO YOU.

NURAY, DO YOU THINK IGD WILL CONSIDER ME A TRAITOR AND COME AFTER ME?

YOU KNOW, WE SHARE A SLOGAN WITH THE FASCISTS: "IF I TURN MY BACK, SHOOT ME TOO."

AND SO MY POLITICAL, ACTIVIST LIFE ENDED LIKE THAT. YOU'RE SEPARATED FROM A WORLD THAT GAVE YOU YOUR WHOLE LIFE. IN AN INSTANT, YOU'RE IN A VACUUM.

Gül

# THE NOTEBOOK

WHEN I WAS 16, I LIVED WITH MY FAMILY IN ISTANBUL. MY BEST FRIEND, BILGE, AND I ATTENDED THE SAME HIGH SCHOOL.

ONE DAY, MY BROTHER GAVE ME A COPY OF THE **COMMUNIST MANIFESTO**.

YOU SHOULD READ THIS. IT'S AN IMPORTANT BOOK. TELL ME WHAT YOU THINK OF IT.

A WEEK LATER.

YOU SHOULD READ THIS, BILGE. IT'S IMPORTANT.

LET'S MEET IN A COUPLE OF DAYS AND DISCUSS IT. DON'T LET MY BROTHER KNOW I LENT IT TO YOU.

A FEW DAYS LATER.

I READ IT, BUT I DON'T SEE THE POINT OF A WORKER'S MOVEMENT. WE DON'T HAVE THAT MANY FACTORIES IN TURKEY.

IT'S NOT NUMBERS. IT'S STRENGTH. OUR LABOR UNIONS ARE STRONG.

THAT EVENING.

PLEASE, BROTHER, CAN'T I TAKE THE BOOK TO SCHOOL? EVERYONE SHOULD READ IT!

I CAN'T GIVE IT TO YOU. IF YOUR TEACHERS SEE IT, YOU'LL GET IN TROUBLE.

I STAYED UP ALL NIGHT AND COPIED THE ENTIRE TEXT INTO A NOTEBOOK.

THE NEXT DAY, I TOOK THE NOTEBOOK TO SCHOOL.

ONE DAY, THE NOTEBOOK WAS MISSING.

A GIRL I DIDN'T KNOW HAD BEEN HANGING AROUND, LISTENING.

I KNOW YOU TOOK IT. GIVE IT BACK!

THE NOTEBOOK WAS NEVER RETURNED.

AFTER GRADUATING FROM HIGH SCHOOL, I ENROLLED IN A TEACHER TRAINING SCHOOL AND BOUGHT MY OWN COPY OF THE *COMMUNIST MANIFESTO.*

I STOOD WITH STUDENTS BOYCOTTING THE SCHOOL. WHEN OTHER STUDENTS LINKED ARMS AND TRIED TO MARCH PAST, WE BARRICADED OURSELVES INSIDE THE BUILDING.

BOYKOT

BOYKOT

GÜL, DID YOU LOCK THE DOOR?

YES.

* BANNER: BOYCOTT! WE DEMAND CHILDCARE

MAY 1, 1977, ISTANBUL, TAKSIM SQUARE

NEARLY HALF A MILLION PEOPLE MARCHED TO TAKSIM SQUARE TO CELEBRATE LABOR DAY. ALTHOUGH SHE WAS PREGNANT, GÜL WORE A RED SCARF AND MARCHED WITH HER UNION.

KA POW!

WHEN THE SHOOTING STARTED, EVERYONE RAN. DOZENS OF PEOPLE WERE KILLED AND NEARLY TWO HUNDRED WOUNDED, MOST CRUSHED IN THE PANIC AFTER POLICE ARRIVED. IT WAS NEVER CLEAR WHO DID THE SHOOTING.

LOOK AT THAT WOMAN IN THE RED SCARF. SHE'S PREGNANT BUT COMING FROM TAKSIM. AWFUL.

HELP US!

THEY'RE SHOOTING!

RUN! RUN!

OH NO, IT'S MY DAUGHTER! GÜL!!

IT GIVES YOU AN EXTRAORDINARY STRENGTH. BELIEVE ME, A PERSON IS MORE POWERFUL THAN AN ATOM BOMB.

## The Factory Owner

THE STRIKES WERE BAD ENOUGH, BOSS. NOW THEY'RE FIRING BULLETS.

IT'S BEEN TWO WEEKS NOW. EVERY DAY THE UNIONS STORM THE FACTORY. THEY SHOUT, THEY KICK PEOPLE, SMASH GLASS.

THERE WERE TWO UNIONS, ONE ASSOCIATED WITH THE MHP* AND THE OTHER WITH THE LEFTISTS. EVERY DAY THERE WAS A PROBLEM. PEOPLE COULDN'T WORK.

COMMUNIST!

FASCIST!

THE FACTORY BELL SOUNDED THE END OF THE WORKDAY.

* MHP: NATIONALIST MOVEMENT PARTY

POWW

YOU KNOW THEY'LL KILL SOMEONE ON THE OTHER SIDE TOMORROW. WHAT CAN WE DO?

I HEAR THAT THE HEAD OF MHP IS COMING TO ISTANBUL TOMORROW. LET'S SEE IF WE CAN GET HIM TO COME HERE AND PUT A STOP TO THIS.

THE FOLLOWING DAY.

NOW TELL ME WHO'S BEHIND THIS.

THE MAN SELLS TEA IN THE BUILDING. THERE'S A NATIONALIST GROUP AND THIS TEA MAN BEHAVES AS IF HE'S THE GANG LEADER. HE'S ALWAYS PROVOKING THEM TO FIGHT.

CALL THE TEA MAN.

WHAT'S HAPPENING HERE?

I'M A NATIONALIST. I ORGANIZE THEM. I'M UNDER YOUR COMMAND.

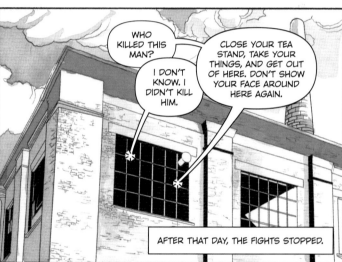

WHO KILLED THIS MAN?

I DON'T KNOW. I DIDN'T KILL HIM.

CLOSE YOUR TEA STAND, TAKE YOUR THINGS, AND GET OUT OF HERE. DON'T SHOW YOUR FACE AROUND HERE AGAIN.

AFTER THAT DAY, THE FIGHTS STOPPED.

THAT EVENING, THE FACTORY OWNER DROVE AROUND HIS HOUSE TWICE BEFORE PARKING THE CAR IN HIS DRIVEWAY.

TWO PROMINENT PEOPLE I KNOW WERE EXECUTED IN THEIR HOMES. LAST MONTH I WAS LOOKING OUT THE WINDOW OF MY OFFICE DOWNTOWN AND SAW PEOPLE BEING MACHINE GUNNED! AND BEFORE THAT THE BUILDING WAS BOMBED.

WHEN WILL THIS END? PEOPLE I KNOW SOLD EVERYTHING AND WENT ABROAD OR SENT THEIR SONS OUT OF THE COUNTRY. WE'VE BECOME ACCUSTOMED TO VIOLENCE. WE'RE ALWAYS AFRAID.

## Nuray

# THE T-SHIRTS

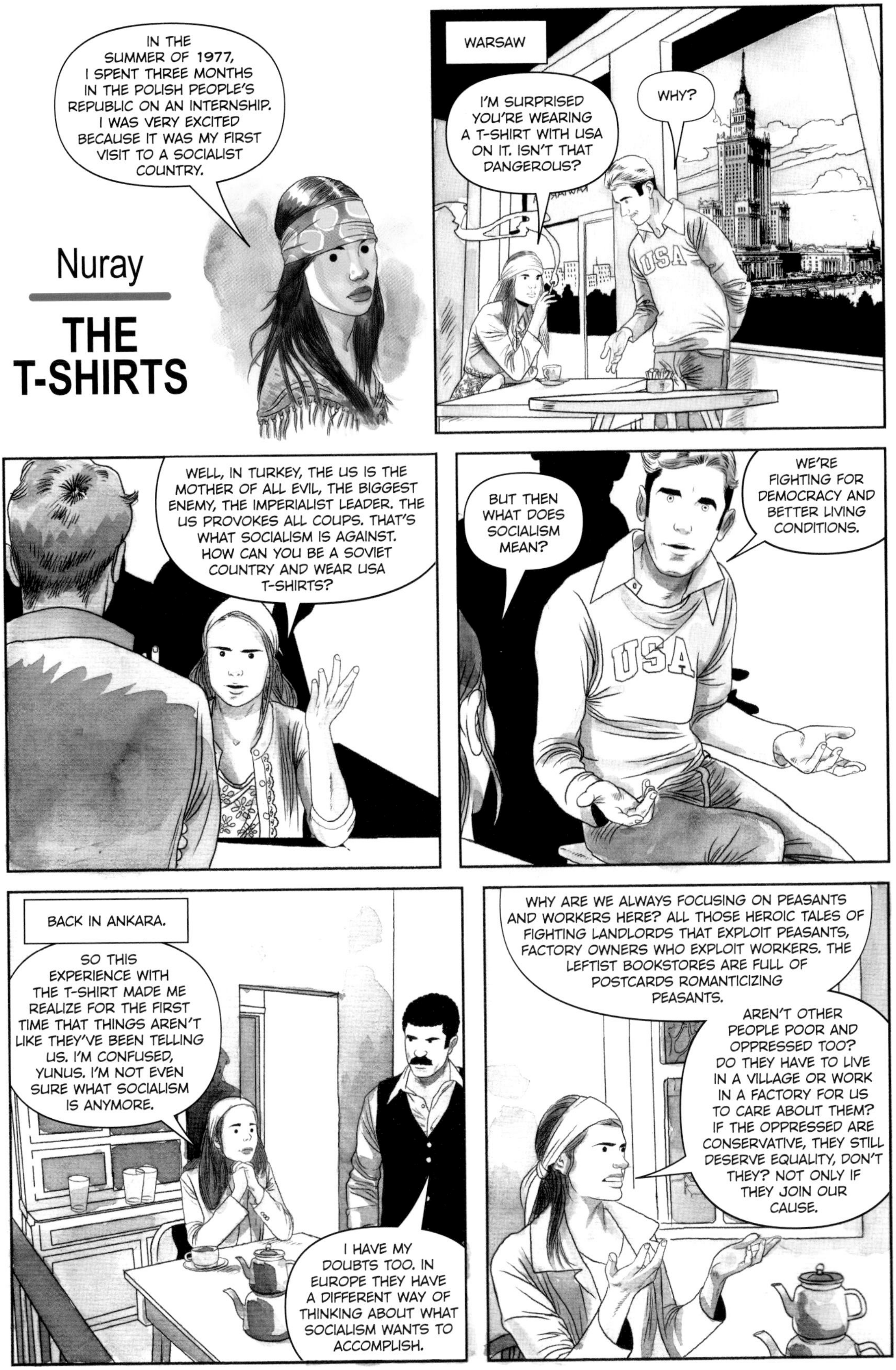

IN THE SUMMER OF 1977, I SPENT THREE MONTHS IN THE POLISH PEOPLE'S REPUBLIC ON AN INTERNSHIP. I WAS VERY EXCITED BECAUSE IT WAS MY FIRST VISIT TO A SOCIALIST COUNTRY.
WARSAW
I'M SURPRISED YOU'RE WEARING A T-SHIRT WITH USA ON IT. ISN'T THAT DANGEROUS?
WHY?
USA
WELL, IN TURKEY, THE US IS THE MOTHER OF ALL EVIL, THE BIGGEST ENEMY, THE IMPERIALIST LEADER. THE US PROVOKES ALL COUPS. THAT'S WHAT SOCIALISM IS AGAINST. HOW CAN YOU BE A SOVIET COUNTRY AND WEAR USA T-SHIRTS?
WE'RE FIGHTING FOR DEMOCRACY AND BETTER LIVING CONDITIONS.
BUT THEN WHAT DOES SOCIALISM MEAN?
USA
BACK IN ANKARA.
SO THIS EXPERIENCE WITH THE T-SHIRT MADE ME REALIZE FOR THE FIRST TIME THAT THINGS AREN'T LIKE THEY'VE BEEN TELLING US. I'M CONFUSED, YUNUS. I'M NOT EVEN SURE WHAT SOCIALISM IS ANYMORE.
I HAVE MY DOUBTS TOO. IN EUROPE THEY HAVE A DIFFERENT WAY OF THINKING ABOUT WHAT SOCIALISM WANTS TO ACCOMPLISH.
WHY ARE WE ALWAYS FOCUSING ON PEASANTS AND WORKERS HERE? ALL THOSE HEROIC TALES OF FIGHTING LANDLORDS THAT EXPLOIT PEASANTS, FACTORY OWNERS WHO EXPLOIT WORKERS. THE LEFTIST BOOKSTORES ARE FULL OF POSTCARDS ROMANTICIZING PEASANTS.
AREN'T OTHER PEOPLE POOR AND OPPRESSED TOO? DO THEY HAVE TO LIVE IN A VILLAGE OR WORK IN A FACTORY FOR US TO CARE ABOUT THEM? IF THE OPPRESSED ARE CONSERVATIVE, THEY STILL DESERVE EQUALITY, DON'T THEY? NOT ONLY IF THEY JOIN OUR CAUSE.

WE'D BETTER KEEP THIS CONVERSATION TO OURSELVES. BEING IN A LEFTIST GROUP IS LIKE BEING IN A TEKKE.* YOU DO WHATEVER THE SHEIKH WANTS. YOU THINK WHAT HE WANTS YOU TO THINK. DON'T LET ANYONE KNOW YOU HAVE THESE QUESTIONS, NURAY. REMEMBER THE SAYING, "DO AS I SAY. IF NOT, YOU'RE A TRAITOR." DON'T DISCUSS THIS EVEN WITH FERIDE.

I HAVE TO GO.

DO YOU STILL HAVE THAT GUN?

IT'S IN MY DRAWER AT THE DORM.

BRING IT TOMORROW. IT'S NOT SOMETHING FOR WOMEN.

## Orhan

# SMALL PUFF OF AIR

THE NEXT DAY IN CLASS.

THERE'S BEEN A CONFLICT.

THE FASCISTS HAVE SHOT OUR FRIEND. THE HOSPITAL URGENTLY NEEDS BLOOD TYPE B.

β Rh+

WHERE ARE YOU GOING?

THAT'S MY BLOOD TYPE.

ARE YOU CRAZY?

* TEKKE: AN ISLAMIC DERVISH LODGE

A BIG, SILENT CROWD OF LEFTIST STUDENTS HAD GATHERED IN THE COURTYARD.

THEY'RE SO QUIET. SOMETHING IS GOING TO HAPPEN!

I DON'T LIKE THIS. LET'S GO.

SUDDENLY, ORHAN HEARD SHOUTS AND GUNSHOTS AS THE POLICE CHARGED THE CROWD.

NURAY!

A BULLET FLIES BY ORHAN'S HEAD, MAKING A SMALL PUFF OF AIR.

BLAM

COME ON. LET'S GET OUT OF HERE.

AT LEAST THREE SHOT. IT'S GOING TO BE WAR.

WHO?

TWO GUYS AND A GIRL.

I HAVE TO GO. IT MIGHT BE NURAY.

ORHAN, COME BACK. DON'T BE CRAZY.

THIRTY MINUTES EARLIER.

## Yunus
### CONSEQUENCES

YUNUS, TAKE IT.

NURAY, LOOK OUT!

BLAM

OF COURSE, I FLUNKED AFTER THIS HAPPENED, THOUGH I GRADUATED IN THE END. I CAN'T SAY ANY MORE. THE ROMANTICISM OF THE LEFT IS DEAD FOR ME.

## Orhan
# ONE DAY

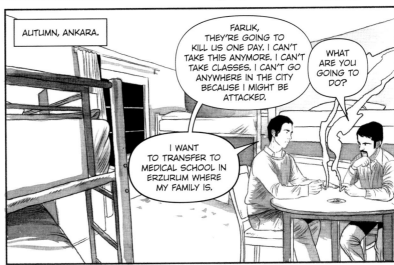

AUTUMN, ANKARA.

FARUK, THEY'RE GOING TO KILL US ONE DAY. I CAN'T TAKE THIS ANYMORE. I CAN'T TAKE CLASSES. I CAN'T GO ANYWHERE IN THE CITY BECAUSE I MIGHT BE ATTACKED.

WHAT ARE YOU GOING TO DO?

I WANT TO TRANSFER TO MEDICAL SCHOOL IN ERZURUM WHERE MY FAMILY IS.

GO SEE THIS GUY IN THE MHP.

A WEEK LATER.

I'VE APPLIED TO THE TEACHER'S SCHOOL IN ISTANBUL. THEY TAKE ONLY TEACHERS AND STUDENTS WHO ARE IDEALIST OR RELIGIOUS. COMMUNISTS CAN'T GET IN; THEY CAN'T PASS THE EXAM.

HE DID IT. YOUR GUY WROTE A LETTER TO THE MHP CHAIRMAN IN ERZURUM. THEY SAID THEY COULD HELP. HOW ABOUT YOU?

WHY NOT?

THEY GET WRONG ANSWERS ON THE HISTORY PART.

SPRING, ISTANBUL.

THE UNIVERSITY TURNED ME DOWN. I HEARD THAT SOME IDEALISTS TRANSFERRED THERE FROM HACETTEPE LAST YEAR AND MADE A SCENE AND PISSED OFF THE PROFESSORS. NOW THEY THINK WE'RE ALL TROUBLEMAKERS. WHAT AM I GOING TO DO?

YOU COULD TAKE THE UNIVERSITY EXAM AGAIN AND GET INTO THE SCHOOL THAT WAY.* I CAN FIND YOU A PLACE TO STAY HERE IN THE MEANTIME.

A YEAR LATER.

YOU DISAPPEARED! SOMEONE TOLD ME YOU WENT HOME TO ERZURUM. WHAT HAPPENED?

I TOOK THE EXAM. I DIDN'T GET INTO MEDICAL SCHOOL, BUT ONLY INTO AGRICULTURE. I QUIT!

I'M GOING TO BE A TEACHER. THE NATION NEEDS TEACHERS AND AGRICULTURAL EXPERTS. DON'T JUST THINK ABOUT YOURSELF.

SO I WON'T BE A DOCTOR. MAYBE I SHOULD GO INTO POLITICS. A POLITICIAN CAN HELP AS MANY PEOPLE AS A DOCTOR.

AND DON'T FORGET--YOU'LL GET RICH!

I WONDER WHAT HAPPENED TO NURAY.

* COMPETITIVE NATIONAL EXAMINATIONS DETERMINE WHAT SUBJECT A STUDENT CAN STUDY AND WHERE.

AH, YOUR NURAY WALKS WITH A LIMP NOW. I HEAR SHE'S GETTING MARRIED.

I GREW UP IN A VILLAGE WITH MY GRANDFATHER, PARENTS, AND SISTER NURAY. WITH MY HIGH EXAM SCORES, I WON A PLACE IN THE GERMAN SCHOOL IN ISTANBUL, SO MY PARENTS SENT ME TO STAY WITH MY GRANDMOTHER. MY ELDER SISTER, BILGE, LIVED THERE TOO.

Fikret

# THE GUIDE

A FEW DAYS A WEEK I SLEPT AT THE SCHOOL. THOSE NIGHTS, I AND SOME OTHER BOYS TOOK OFF OUR UNIFORMS AND SCHOOL PINS AND DISCOVERED THE CITY.

HOW ABOUT GOING TO THE CINEMA THIS WEEKEND?

IN SCHOOL, WE READ BERTHOLD BRECHT AND LEARNED TO DISPUTE AND APPROACH SUBJECTS FROM DIFFERENT SIDES.

DOES GOD EXIST?

ARE MEN AND WOMEN DIFFERENT?

DOES MORALITY EXIST OR NOT?

WHAT'S GOING ON?

THEY JUST CAME BACK FROM THE ROOF.

WHAT'S ON THE ROOF?

THE GERMAN ASTRONOMY TEACHER. HE SENT FOR TELESCOPES AND SPECIAL STUFF FROM GERMANY, AND SET THEM UP ON THE ROOF. TWICE A WEEK HE COMES TO SCHOOL IN THE EVENING. HE CHOOSES THE BEST STUDENTS IN HIS CLASS AND TAKES THEM UP THERE TO WATCH THE STARS.

I NEVER FORGOT HIM TELLING US ABOUT THE STARS, LIKE A DREAM.

A FEW YEARS LATER, WHEN I WAS A STUDENT AT ISTANBUL UNIVERSITY, I LISTENED TO THE DEAN GIVE A SPEECH.

HE'S NOT ONE OF THOSE MEN WHO'D WATCH STARS ON THE ROOF. HE'S JUST AN ORDINARY MAN.

THE BEST THING THAT HAPPENED TO ME IN MY FIRST YEAR AT UNIVERSITY WAS LEFTISM. IT BEGAN LIKE THIS: I WAS IN A THEATER PLAY ABOUT THE NAZI REGIME AND A COURTROOM.

I LEARNED ABOUT DIALECTICS IN HIGH SCHOOL COMPOSITION CLASS. IT MEANS YOU DON'T DEFEND AN IDEA WITHOUT FIRST TALKING ABOUT THE OPPOSITE IDEA.

THIS IS A LEFTIST PLAY. IT'S ABOUT DIALECTICS.

SO, WHAT WE LEARNED WAS ACTUALLY LEFTISM.

SO, FIKRET, I HEAR YOU JOINED DEV-GENÇ.*

THERE ARE SO MANY GROUPS, BROTHER. DEV-GENÇ SEEMED MIDDLE OF THE ROAD, NOT IN THE SOVIET OR CHINESE STREAK.

IN THE MORNING, I WAS CALLED TO A DEV-GENÇ FORUM.

AMERICA INVADED...

THE FASCISTS SHOT ....

IT'S ALWAYS ABOUT THE SAME THINGS. I'M GOING TO MY PHILOSOPHY CLASS.

* DEV-GENÇ: REVOLUTIONARY YOUTH FEDERATION OF TURKEY

AFTER CLASS, I RAN INTO MY DEV-GENÇ LEADER IN THE HALL.

I SAW YOU LEAVE THE FORUM THIS MORNING. IS THERE SOMETHING YOU WANT TO TALK ABOUT?

THERE IS. MARXISM IS SAID TO BE INVOLVED IN EVERYTHING, YET IT DOESN'T HAVE A SINGLE THING TO SAY ABOUT THE PROFESSION WE'RE LEARNING. I'M NOT DOUBTING WHAT DEV-GENÇ SAYS. IT'S JUST THAT I'M SO BORED.

HERE, READ THIS. IN *BİRİKİM* THEY WRITE ABOUT THINGS WE DON'T TALK ABOUT HERE-- EUROPEAN COMMUNISM, THE LIBERTARIAN LEFT. FOR ME, READING IT IS LIKE BREATHING. YOUR PROBLEM IS THAT YOU'RE NOT CRITICAL OF YOUR OWN LEFTISM.

I DIDN'T THINK THAT WAS ALLOWED.

THERE ARE PEOPLE WHOSE HEADS WORK IN THINKING, BUT NOT IN POLITICS. OTHERS ARE READY TO DO ANYTHING, BUT HAVE NO BRAIN. THIS MAGAZINE WILL MAKE THOSE WHO DO POLITICS GET USED TO THINKING.

SO THEY'LL READ THAT INSTEAD OF JOINING SOME SHIT GROUP AND GETTING KILLED.

IT WAS A STRANGE, DIVIDED WORLD. AND HOME WAS AN ALTOGETHER DIFFERENT WORLD, AN ORDINARY LIFE. NEITHER CLASSES NOR LEFTISM EXISTED THERE. WE READ A LOT ABOUT MARXISM, BUT NO TRACE OF IT EXISTED.

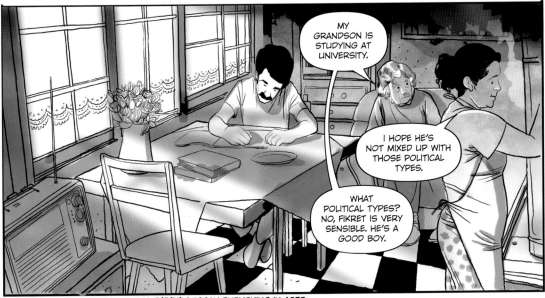

MY GRANDSON IS STUDYING AT UNIVERSITY.

I HOPE HE'S NOT MIXED UP WITH THOSE POLITICAL TYPES.

WHAT POLITICAL TYPES? NO, FIKRET IS VERY SENSIBLE. HE'S A GOOD BOY.

\* THE SOCIALIST CULTURE MAGAZINE *BİRİKİM* BEGAN PUBLISHING IN 1975.

93

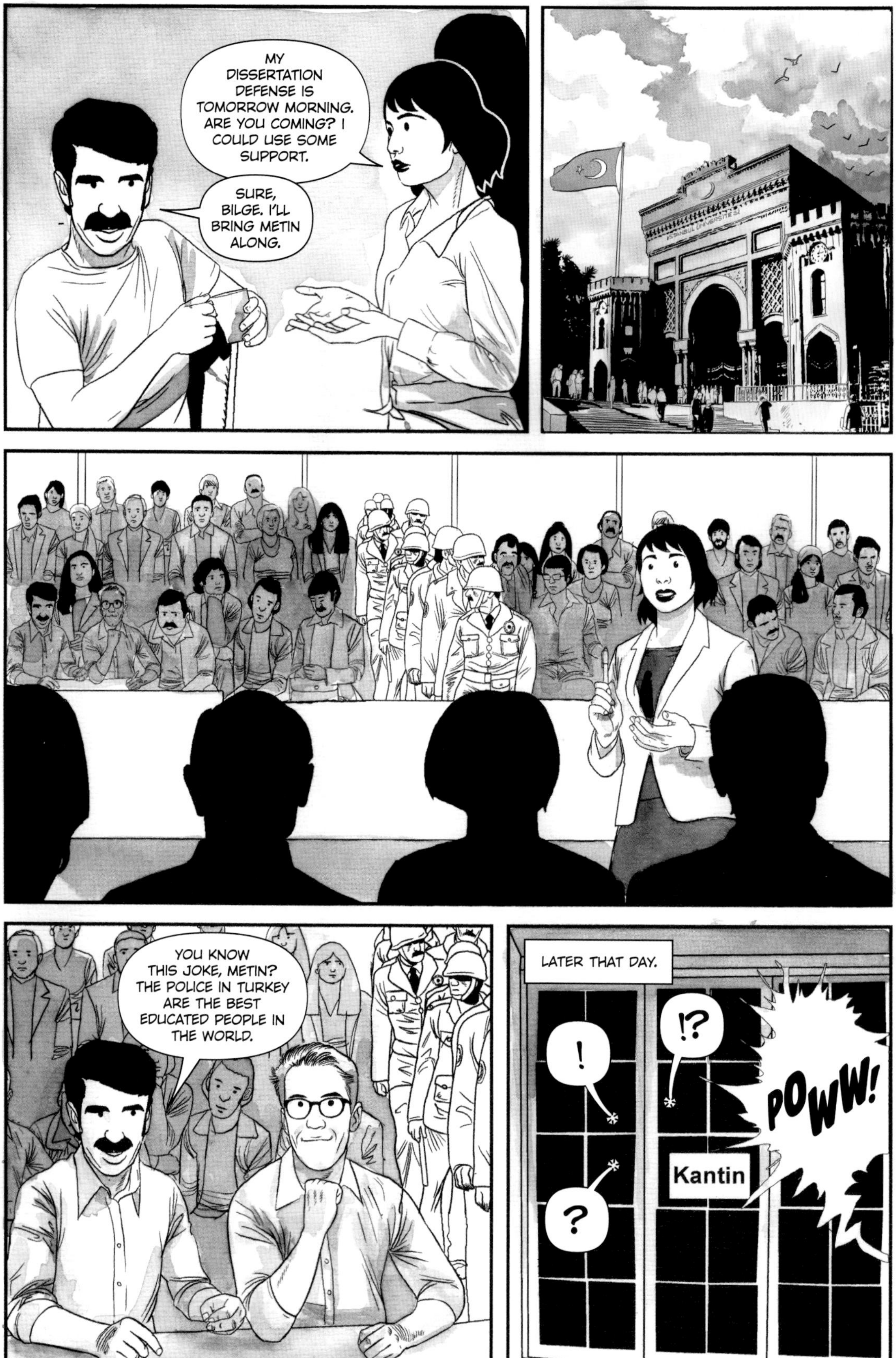
MY DISSERTATION DEFENSE IS TOMORROW MORNING. ARE YOU COMING? I COULD USE SOME SUPPORT.
SURE, BILGE. I'LL BRING METIN ALONG.
YOU KNOW THIS JOKE, METIN? THE POLICE IN TURKEY ARE THE BEST EDUCATED PEOPLE IN THE WORLD.
LATER THAT DAY.
!
!?
?
Kantin
POWW!

* KANTIN: CAFETERIA

WHAT HAPPENED?

THEY KILLED LITTLE HIKMET.

MINI HIKMET? THE FASCIST? HE'S SO DUMB, WHY WOULD SOMEONE KILL HIM?

HE CAME TO CAMPUS WITH A GUN AND WAS SHOWING IT TO THE LEFTIST GUYS. IS THAT STUPID OR WHAT? THEY EVENTUALLY TOOK HIM OUT.

A HUNDRED ARMED FASCISTS, MEMBERS OF THE GRAY WOLVES, GATHERED IN FRONT OF THE SCHOOL, BLOCKING PEOPLE FROM GOING INSIDE.

THEY'RE NOT FROM OUR SCHOOL, SO THEY HAVE NO IDEA WHO'S LEFTIST AND WHO ISN'T. THEY CAN'T TELL US APART.

THE NEXT MORNING.

I HAVE BAD NEWS. THE FASCISTS RETALIATED. THEY KIDNAPPED METIN.

WE HAVE TO RESCUE HIM.

THE POLICE ARE LOOKING. THEY'LL FIND HIM.

I'M SICK OF THIS BECOMING SO ROUTINE. SOME GUY IN ANKARA TOOK MY SISTER NURAY TO A DEMONSTRATION AND SHE WAS SHOT.

A DAY LATER.

THE POLICE FOUND METIN'S BODY IN ONE OF THE SLUMS.

THE FASCISTS KILLED HIM.

THEY CUT EVERY PART OF HIS BODY, HIS FACE, HIS NOSE.

POLITICS WILL KILL US ALL.

AFTER NURAY GOT OUT OF THE HOSPITAL, SHE AND YUNUS WERE MARRIED.

Ankara
1979

**WEDDING**

ONLY FRIENDS AND FAMILY ATTENDED THE WEDDING PARTY. THERE WAS NO FUEL FOR PEOPLE'S CARS.

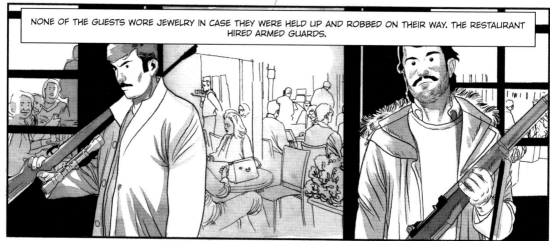

NONE OF THE GUESTS WORE JEWELRY IN CASE THEY WERE HELD UP AND ROBBED ON THEIR WAY. THE RESTAURANT HIRED ARMED GUARDS.

I'M MISSING MY USUAL FRIDAY MEETING WITH MY FRIENDS. WE ALL WERE EDUCATED TOGETHER, YOU KNOW, BUT IN MY DAY THERE WERE NO WORKING WOMEN. THERE'S ALWAYS A COMPETITION OVER WHO MAKES THE BEST FOOD. WE GIVE THE LEFTOVERS TO THE DOORKEEPER. OUR DOORKEEPER IS A WOMAN. HER HUSBAND WORKS IN THE FLOUR FACTORY. HE'S OFFICIALLY THE DOORKEEPER, BUT HIS WIFE DOES THE WORK. SHE HAS BAD KNEES.

WELL, THAT'S THE PROBLEM WITH CAPITALISM. WE EXPLOIT THE WORKERS AND THEN, NATURALLY, THE MALE WORKERS EXPLOIT THE WOMEN.

IN MY DAY, WOMEN NEVER TALKED POLITICS. WE TALKED ABOUT CHILDREN. WE READ NEWSPAPERS. WE HAD A TELEVISION. THE NEIGHBORS CAME AND WATCHED AFTER DINNER. WE HAD BOXSEATS AT THE CINEMA. WE WENT ABROAD. IT WAS A GOOD LIFE.

AUNTIE, YOU'RE LIVING ON A DIFFERENT PLANET THAN THE REST OF US.

COME ON, COME TO US!

DO YOU KNOW WHERE WE CAN GET LIGHTBULBS, SUGAR, TOILET PAPER? THERE'S NOTHING IN THE GROCERY SHOPS. THIS MORNING, I SUCKED THROUGH A HOSE TO GET GAS FROM A FRIEND'S FUEL TANK.

THAT'S THE LAST RESORT WHEN YOU RUN OUT OF RAKI.

HA HA HA! HA HA HA HA HA!

MMM!..

HA HA!

LAST WEEK, THERE WAS A SHOOTING IN MY NEIGHBORHOOD. WE WERE SCARED. THE WOMEN ALL HAD DRIVERS TO TAKE THEM HOME. EVERYONE DRIVES AROUND WITH A CLUB IN THE CAR TO DEFEND THEMSELVES. EVERYONE. THE DOORKEEPER TOLD US THAT HER SON ONLY HAS A PRIMARY SCHOOL EDUCATION BECAUSE IT'S TOO DANGEROUS FOR HIM TO GO TO SCHOOL. CAN YOU IMAGINE?

YOU NEEDN'T WORRY, AUNTIE. LOOK, UNCLE HAS A CAR. HE'LL TAKE YOU HOME.

FIKRET, YOU'RE LEAVING ALREADY? THE CURFEW ISN'T FOR ANOTHER TWO HOURS.

I'M MEETING SOME FRIENDS AT A FISH RESTAURANT.

WHAT ABOUT THE CURFEW?

FROM THERE WE GO TO A FRIEND'S HOUSE TO SMOKE HASH AND PLAY SOME ANTIFASCISM GUITAR. SO I'LL BE IN SOMEONE'S HOME BEFORE CURFEW, I'M JUST NOT SURE WHOSE.

PEOPLE LEFT EARLY. THE STREETS WERE DARK AND YOU HAD TO BE HOME BEFORE THE CURFEW. IT WAS A JOYLESS WEDDING.

## September 12, 1980

## COUP D'ÉTAT

WE ARE DISSOLVING THE GOVERNMENT AND IMPOSING MARTIAL LAW.

...OUR NATION IS IN NEED OF NATIONAL UNITY AND SOLIDARITY.

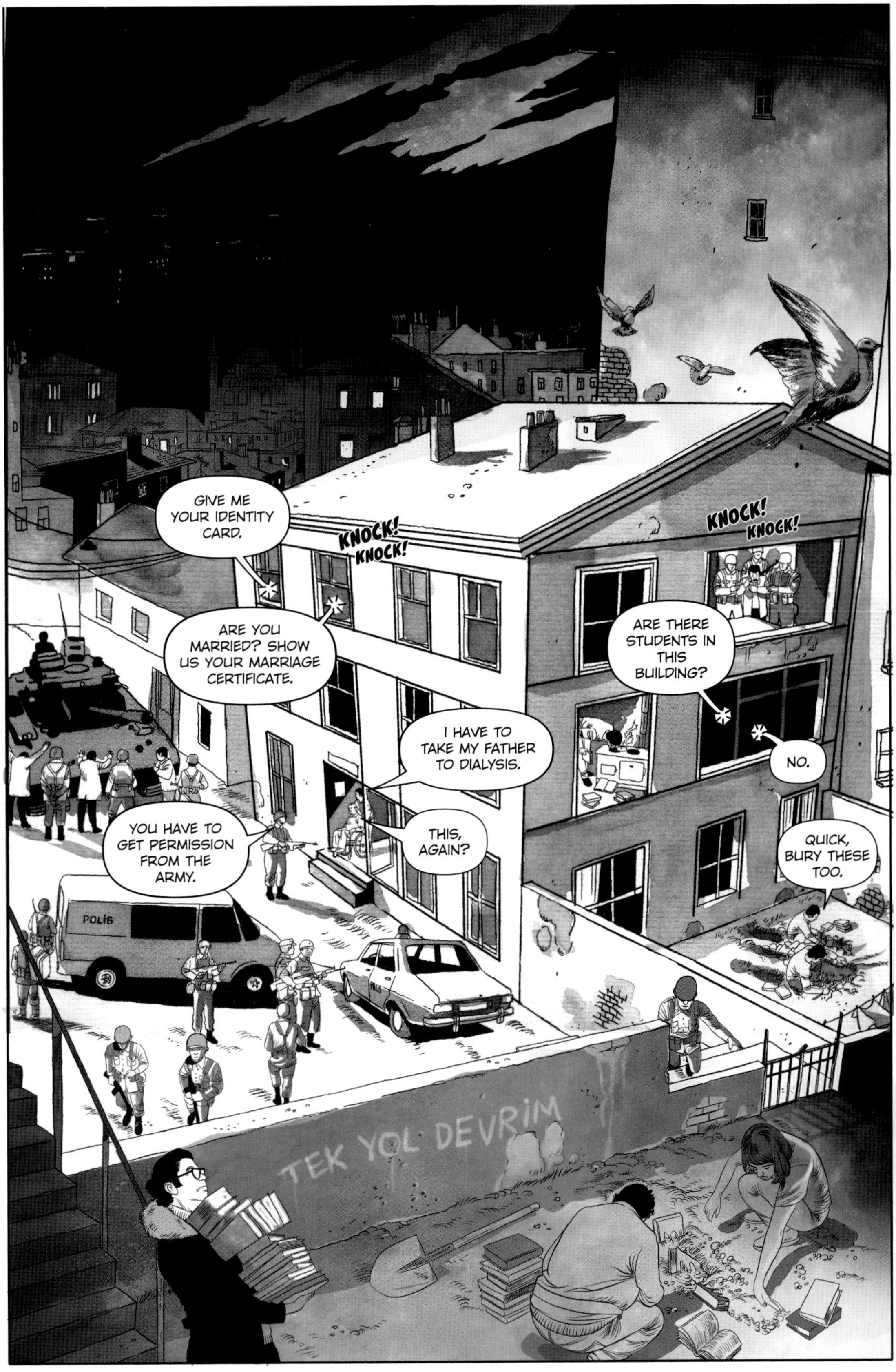
GIVE ME YOUR IDENTITY CARD.
KNOCK! KNOCK!
ARE YOU MARRIED? SHOW US YOUR MARRIAGE CERTIFICATE.
KNOCK! KNOCK!
ARE THERE STUDENTS IN THIS BUILDING?
NO.
I HAVE TO TAKE MY FATHER TO DIALYSIS.
THIS, AGAIN?
YOU HAVE TO GET PERMISSION FROM THE ARMY.
QUICK, BURY THESE TOO.
POLIS
TEK YOL DEVRIM

## Nuray

NURAY AND YUNUS HAD MOVED TO ISTANBUL.

ANKARA IS A DARK, FILTHY CITY, A THING LIKE A NIGHTMARE. I DON'T WANT TO REMEMBER IT. THE CITY OF DEATH. GOVERNMENT BUILDINGS, HUGE STATUES. ISTANBUL IS MORE COSMOPOLITAN AND IT HAS THE BOSPHORUS.

BUT NOW EVERYONE IS AFRAID.

THEY'RE LOOKING FOR ME.

FIKRET TOLD ME IF THE POLICE DON'T FIND A PERSON, THEY PUT THE FILE ON THE BOTTOM AND NOTHING HAPPENS FOR TEN MONTHS.

WHERE CAN WE GO?

## Gül

GÜL WAS IN HER FATHER'S APARTMENT. HER HUSBAND ESCAPED OUT THE BACK.

THEY'VE COME TO GET ME. WHAT WILL HAPPEN TO MY CHILDREN?

SHE REMEMBERED WHEN THEY DISCOVERED A COLLEAGUE'S BODY.

RNNNGGG

RNNNGGG

OPEN THE DOOR, MY DAUGHTER, THEY'VE COME.

NO, BABA, IT'S JUST THE NEIGHBOR. HE'S JUST DRUNK AGAIN.

## Feride

RNNNGGG

FERIDE.
FERIDE!

WELCOME, COUSIN. GO IN THE BACK ROOM.

DID ANYONE FOLLOW YOU?

KNOCK
KNOCK

!?

FERIDE, OPEN UP. IT'S NURAY.

KNOCK
KNOCK

THEY'VE TAKEN YUNUS.

I WAS CAUGHT WRITING GRAFFITI AND ARRESTED. I WAS TORTURED. THEY LET ME GO BECAUSE I HAD NO GUNS.

THEY BEAT ME ON MY HANDS, MY FEET.

I CAN'T GO BACK IN THERE.

101

I LOST MY FRIENDS. IT AFFECTS EVERYTHING.

I KNOW. MY SISTER BILGE'S LIFE CHANGED. IT WAS CUT LIKE A KNIFE. SHE CHANGED ALL HER FRIENDS.

THE SOLDIERS ARE HANGING OUR GUYS. I WANT TO HANG. WHY AM I LIVING?

DON'T TALK LIKE THAT! STRANGE MEN ARE WALKING BACK AND FORTH IN FRONT OF THE BUILDING. YOU HAVE TO LEAVE RIGHT NOW.

## Yunus

TELL US THE OTHER NAMES.

THUMP!

ZZZTT!..

AAAAH!

I CAN'T TAKE THE PAIN. WHAT IF I SAY FAKE NAMES?

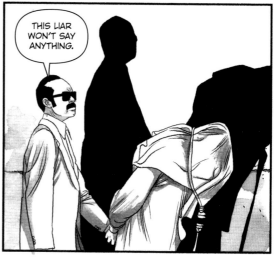

THIS LIAR WON'T SAY ANYTHING.

THEY BLINDFOLDED HIM AND DROVE HIM AROUND IN A CAR.

WE'LL KILL YOU.

UGGH!

THUD!

FARUK VISITED ORHAN AT HIS PARENTS' HOME IN ERZURUM.

WE ARE IN NEED OF NATIONAL UNITY AND SOLIDARITY...

I DON'T WANT TO CAUSE YOU ANY TROUBLE, BUT THANK YOU FOR LETTING ME STAY HERE.

HOW IS YOUR FAMILY?

MY SON, ANY FRIEND OF ORHAN'S IS WELCOME HERE.

MY FATHER IS ILL. HE'S MHP, BUT I DON'T THINK HIS HEART WOULD SURVIVE A POLICE RAID.

## Faruk

I'D BE PROUD TO BE A MARTYR FOR OUR NATION, BUT I DON'T UNDERSTAND WHY THEY'RE AFTER ME. THIS IS OUR COUP. IT'S AGAINST THE COMMUNISTS. WHY ARE THEY ALSO HANGING MHP* GUYS?

I THOUGHT ARMY OFFICERS ARE SUPPOSED TO BE ABOVE POLITICS.

KNOCK! KNOCK!

## Fikret

WHEN THEY ANNOUNCED MARTIAL LAW, WE WERE RELIEVED.

ISTANBUL, A FEW WEEKS AFTER THE COUP.

GREAT, NOW I CAN GET MY MEDICAL DEGREE. I'M SO FED UP WITH BOYCOTTS, FORUMS, DISRUPTED CLASSES.

IT'S A BEAUTIFUL DAY.

YOU WERE ALWAYS OUT FRONT WAVING THE BANNER.

RUNNING FROM THE POLICE, I REALIZED HOW MUCH I'VE MISSED DOING SPORTS.

HA HA HA

* THE MILITARY GOVERNMENT CHARGED MEMBERS OF THE MHP AND AFFILIATED ORGANIZATIONS LIKE THE GRAY WOLVES WITH HUNDREDS OF MURDERS.

I MISS GOOD THEATER. MAYBE I'LL JOIN A THEATER GROUP.

May 2012
Istanbul

**IDEALS**

ONE OF YOUR FRESH SIMITS, PLEASE.

ELEKTRİK
UYDU SİSTEMLERİ

FIRIN

SELAM ALEIKUM, MY BROTHER.

ALEIKUM SELAM, FARUK BEY. WHAT DO YOU NEED?

A LIGHTBULB, PLEASE.

ALLAH HAS BLESSED US WITH EXCELLENT WEATHER.

IF HE BLESSES US WITH PROSPERITY, I WON'T MIND IF IT RAINS.

ENJOY THE WEATHER, FARUK BEY!

ELEKTRİK
UYD... ...TEMLER

TLF: 02...
GSM: 053...

GOOD THAT YOU'RE BACK, MEHMET. I'M ABOUT TO BEAT YOU.

RIN

ORHAN? IS IT YOU?

FARUK?

I HARDLY RECOGNIZED YOU WITH THAT BEARD. HOW LONG HAS IT BEEN? AT LEAST 35 YEARS! I DIDN'T KNOW WHAT HAPPENED TO YOU AFTER THE COUP.

AH, YOU LOOK THE SAME, STILL THAT DREAMY-EYED IDEALIST GUY, BUT WITH MORE FLESH ON YOUR BONES. DID YOU MARRY YOUR MIHRIBAN?

NO, BUT I'M MARRIED. I HAVE A DAUGHTER, MIRAY, AND THIS IS MY SON, ALP.

HE'S GETTING HIS DOCTORATE IN POLITICAL SCIENCE IN AMERICA. WHY DON'T YOU COME TO DINNER? HE'S HOME FOR THE SUMMER. OR IS YOUR FAMILY WAITING FOR YOU?

THIS IS MY DAUGHTER, EBRU.

I'M ON MY WAY TO VISIT HER IN ÜMRANIYE.

THANKS BE TO GOD.

YOU'LL COME ANOTHER TIME. TELL ME ABOUT YOUR LIFE SINCE WE LAST MET.

THEY ARRESTED ME. MY FATHER PASSED AWAY WHILE I WAS IN PRISON.

I'M SO SORRY.

THE PERSON WHO CAME OUT WASN'T THE SAME PERSON WHO WENT IN. MY SISTER LIVES IN GERMANY. I MARRIED, BUT MY WIFE PASSED AWAY. SINCE THEN, I'VE BEEN TAKING CARE OF MY MOTHER.

AH AH.

DO YOU REMEMBER THE LEFTIST I SHOT DURING A STREET BATTLE? THE ONE WHO DIED.

YES.

YOU REMEMBER THAT I STAYED BESIDE HIM WHEN HE PASSED AWAY. I NEVER TOLD THIS TO ANYONE. BEFORE HE DIED, HE STARTED RECITING THE SHAHADA.*

* SHAHADA: THE ISLAMIC DECLARATION OF BELIEF

THAT WAS A LONG TIME AGO.

ALL THOSE COMMUNISTS WERE SUPPOSED TO BE ATHEISTS. IT STILL HAUNTS ME, THAT WHEN HE THOUGHT HE WAS GOING TO DIE, HE TESTIFIED HIS BELIEF IN ALLAH.

I TRANSFERRED TO A TEACHER'S SCHOOL. BUT RIGHT AFTER I STARTED THERE, THE IDEALIST TEACHERS WERE TRANSFERRED OUT AND REPLACED BY LEFTISTS. ONE NIGHT, A BOMB WENT OFF IN A CLASSROOM. A TEACHER WAS WOUNDED. ANOTHER WAS KNIFED. THERE WAS A DRIVE-BY SHOOTING AT THE TEACHERS' ASSOCIATION AND A TEACHER WAS KILLED. I WAS NEVER ABLE TO GRADUATE.

EVERY TIME THE GOVERNMENT CHANGED...

EVERYTHING ELSE CHANGED, DOWN TO THE GUY BRINGING THE TEA. LEFT AND RIGHT. I NEVER KNEW WHAT THAT ACTUALLY MEANT, THOUGH I KNOW WELL WHAT THEY DID. WHAT WE DID. WELL, I PAID THE PRICE.

I'M SORRY FOR THAT. I'M A DOCTOR NOW WITH A SMALL PRACTICE IN ÜSKÜDAR. YOU SHOULD HAVE BEEN A DOCTOR.

SO YOU STUCK TO MEDICINE. GOOD FOR YOU. YOU ALWAYS KNEW WHAT YOU WANTED.

I HAVE YOU TO THANK. THE MHP GUY YOU SENT ME TO, HE PULLED STRINGS AND GOT ME INTO ERZURUM MEDICAL SCHOOL AFTER ALL. HOW ABOUT YOU?

I WORK A LITTLE AT THIS AND THAT. I HAVE A SMALL PENSION. MY LIFE REVOLVES AROUND THE TARIKAT* NOW. I CAN DO A LOT OF GOOD THAT WAY. AS MUCH AS A DOCTOR, I'D SAY.

* TARIKAT: AN ISLAMIC BROTHERHOOD

109

## Mehmet

### THE ELECTRICIAN

YOU KNOW, ALI, THAT BEARDED GUY, HE WAS A FASCIST BEFORE. NOW HE'S A RELIGIOUS. I WAS JUST A KID IN THOSE DAYS, BUT I REMEMBER THE FIGHTS. AT MY HIGH SCHOOL, THE DEV-SOLISTS* FOUGHT THE DEV-YOLISTS.**

YOU'RE ONE OF THEM!

NO, I'M ONE OF YOU.

WE HELD AN ELECTION IN THE SCHOOL AND MY GROUP OF FRIENDS AND ANOTHER GROUP ATTACKED EACH OTHER.

NO, I'M THE LEADER.

I'M THE LEADER.

IF YOU'RE LEFTIST, YOU STAY WITH THEM. IF YOU'RE RIGHTIST, YOU STAY ON THEIR SIDE.

* DEV-SOL: REVOLUTIONARY LEFT
** DEV-YOL: REVOLUTIONARY PATH

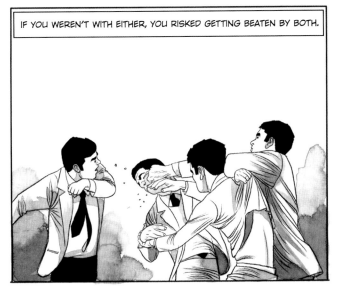

IF YOU WEREN'T WITH EITHER, YOU RISKED GETTING BEATEN BY BOTH.

BETTER YET IS NOT TO BE THERE AT ALL. LIKE THE CHINESE BOOK BY SUN SAYS, "WAR IS AN ART."

I HATE READING, BUT THIS BOOK IS VERY THIN, LIKE MY FINGER.

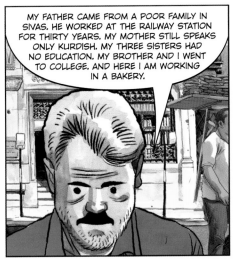

MY FATHER CAME FROM A POOR FAMILY IN SIVAS. HE WORKED AT THE RAILWAY STATION FOR THIRTY YEARS. MY MOTHER STILL SPEAKS ONLY KURDISH. MY THREE SISTERS HAD NO EDUCATION. MY BROTHER AND I WENT TO COLLEGE. AND HERE I AM WORKING IN A BAKERY.

WHAT I MOST REMEMBER ABOUT THE 1970S IS THAT FISH WERE FREE. THERE WERE SO MANY FISH IN THE BOSPHORUS! YOU JUST STICK IN A NET AND IT COMES OUT FULL.

IN THOSE DAYS, IF WE HAD SOME MONEY, WE'D GO TO THE PUB AND DRINK BEER, THEN WE'D HAVE TO WALK HOME BECAUSE WE DIDN'T HAVE ENOUGH MONEY FOR THE BUS. BUT WE WEREN'T INVOLVED IN POLITICS. MY FATHER WOULD BREAK MY HEAD. THIS ISN'T HOW WE WERE RAISED. NO ONE CARED THAT WE WERE KURDS. WE WERE POOR, THAT'S ALL.

IN MY LAST YEAR OF HIGH SCHOOL, A FRIEND WENT TO THE BEACH IN TARABYA WITH HIS FAMILY AND HIS SISTERS. AS HE CAME OUT OF THE WATER, TWO GROUPS CAME AND FOUGHT EACH OTHER RIGHT THERE.

THEY SHOT HIM.

SO I DON'T CARE ABOUT POLITICS. I WENT HOME WHEN IT GOT DARK.

WE'RE TRADESMEN. WE'RE BUSY EARNING OUR BREAD. MAYBE IF WE HAD WORKED IN A FACTORY, WE'D HAVE BECOME LEFTISTS.

I DON'T KNOW WHY IF YOU BECOME A WORKER, YOU BECOME A LEFTIST OR RIGHTIST. IF YOU ASK ME, THERE WAS SOMEONE DIRECTING THEM.

OR RIGHTISTS.

WHO?

IF ONLY WE KNEW. WE DON'T KNOW WHICH CRAZY THREW THE STONE IN THE WELL.

One year later.

June 13, 2013, Gezi Park

PROTESTERS GATHERED TO STOP THE GOVERNMENT FROM TEARING DOWN THE SYCAMORE TREES IN ISTANBUL'S GEZİ PARK TO BUILD A MALL.

THE PRIME MINISTER WARNED:
OUR PATIENCE IS AT AN END.
I AM WARNING YOU FOR THE
LAST TIME. I SAY TO THE
MOTHERS AND FATHERS, PLEASE
TAKE YOUR CHILDREN IN HAND
AND BRING THEM OUT.

KALEIDOSCOPE
FARUK IS VISITING HIS DAUGHTER IN ÜMRANIYE.
LOOK AT ALL THE TEAR GAS, BABA. WHY IS THERE SO MUCH VIOLENCE WHENEVER PEOPLE DEMONSTRATE?
THOSE POLICE ARE OUR HEROES, DEAR EBRU. WHEN THE NATION IS ON FIRE, THEY'RE THE FIRE BRIGADE.
BUT, BABA, WHY NOT JUST LET PEOPLE WALK AND CHANT THEIR SLOGANS AND THEN GO HOME?
IF WE LET THEM, THERE WOULD BE CHAOS.
THE END

# REFLECTIONS

## Ebru

EBRU, DAUGHTER OF FARUK, LIVES IN AN APARTMENT BUILDING IN A WORKING-CLASS DISTRICT OF ISTANBUL. HER HUSBAND IS A BUTCHER WITH HIS OWN SMALL SHOP. THEY LIVE ON ONE FLOOR OF THE BUILDING. HIS THREE BROTHERS LIVE ON THE OTHER FLOORS WITH THEIR FAMILIES, AND HIS PARENTS ON THE GROUND FLOOR. THE FAMILY IS CONSERVATIVE, SO EBRU COVERED HER HEAD WHEN SHE MARRIED. HER MOTHER, WHO DIED WHEN EBRU WAS SEVENTEEN, HAD STOOD FIRM AGAINST HER HUSBAND'S WISH THAT HIS DAUGHTER SHOULD VEIL. EBRU WONDERS SOMETIMES IF HER MOTHER WOULD HAVE APPROVED OF HER CHOICES. EBRU WAS A SECRETARY AT THE LOCAL ISLAMIST MAYOR'S OFFICE, FELL IN LOVE WITH THE MAYOR'S ASSISTANT, AND MARRIED HIM DESPITE HER FATHER'S MISGIVINGS ABOUT HIS EXTREMIST VIEWS. SOON AFTER THEIR MARRIAGE, A DIFFERENT PARTY WON THE LOCAL ELECTIONS AND HER HUSBAND LOST HIS JOB. HIS BROTHERS HELPED HIM SET UP A BUTCHER SHOP. NOW EBRU WORKS AS A SECRETARY AT A COMPANY THAT MANUFACTURES HEADSCARVES. DESPITE TAKING MANAGEMENT TRAINING COURSES, SHE HASN'T MOVED UP IN THE COMPANY, WHICH PREFERS THEIR FEMALE PUBLIC REPRESENTATIVES TO BE UNCOVERED. SHE IS PREGNANT AND WORRIES THAT WHEN THE BABY IS BORN HER HUSBAND'S FAMILY WILL REQUIRE HER TO QUIT HER JOB AND STAY HOME LIKE HER SISTERS-IN-LAW. ONE OF HER BROTHERS-IN-LAW HAS BEEN ARRESTED, ACCUSED OF BEING A FETÖ TERRORIST. NO ONE UNDERSTANDS WHY; HE WAS JUST A SCHOOLTEACHER. THE WHOLE FAMILY IS NERVOUS, WORRIED THAT THEY WILL BE NEXT. EBRU SUSPECTS THAT THEIR NEIGHBOR DENOUNCED HIM TO THE POLICE IN REVENGE OVER AN ARGUMENT. SHE DOESN'T SEE HER FATHER VERY OFTEN AND MISSES HER MOTHER.

## Eylem

EYLEM IS THE DAUGHTER OF YUNUS AND NURAY. SHE STUDIED SOCIOLOGY AT ISTANBUL UNIVERSITY, THEN OPENED A SHOP WITH CAFE IN THE HIPSTER GALATA DISTRICT, SELLING CLOTHING MADE OF TRADITIONAL CLOTH, HANDMADE SLIPPERS, AND OLIVE OIL SOAP. SHE DESIGNS THE CLOTHES AND HIRES WOMEN TO SEW THEM IN THEIR HOMES. EYLEM ALSO TEACHES YOGA AND BLOGS ABOUT BEEKEEPING AND ENVIRONMENTAL GARDENING. SHE LIVES IN A SMALL APARTMENT IN THE CIHANGIR DISTRICT NEAR HER PARENTS. SINCE THE GEZI PROTESTS, SHE HAS DEVELOPED A BRONCHIAL CONDITION, WHICH SHE ATTRIBUTES TO THE TEAR GAS USED BY THE POLICE, SO SHE KEEPS AWAY FROM DEMONSTRATIONS. LAST YEAR, THOUGH, SHE TRAVELED TO AN ANATOLIAN VILLAGE TO SUPPORT BEEKEEPERS WHOSE LIVELIHOOD WAS THREATENED BY A PLAN TO BUILD ELECTRICITY-GENERATING DAMS ON THEIR RIVER THAT WOULD DESTROY ECOTOURISM IN THE AREA. EYLEM DREAMS OF EXPANDING HER BUSINESS AND TRAVELING ABROAD.

# REFLECTIONS

## Alp

ALP IS THE SON OF ORHAN AND BINGÜL, THE WIFE THAT ORHAN'S FAMILY IN ERZURUM CHOSE FOR HIM. ALP'S MOTHER FINISHED HIGH SCHOOL, WEARS A HEADSCARF, AND PRAYS AT HOME FIVE TIMES A DAY. SHE IS AN EXCELLENT COOK. SHE MADE SURE THAT HER CHILDREN DID WELL IN SCHOOL AND LET THEM CHOOSE THEIR OWN PATHS IN LIFE, AS LONG AS THAT INCLUDED GETTING MARRIED AND HAVING CHILDREN. ALP DID WELL ENOUGH ON HIS NATIONAL EXAMS TO STUDY MEDICINE BUT DECIDED INSTEAD TO STUDY POLITICAL SCIENCE. AFTERWARD, HE WAS ACCEPTED INTO A DOCTORAL PROGRAM IN THE UNITED STATES. HE IS ENGAGED TO A FELLOW GRADUATE STUDENT, AN AMERICAN WOMAN, AND THEY ARE VISITING HIS FAMILY IN ISTANBUL TO ANNOUNCE THEIR WEDDING. ALP PLANS TO STAY IN THE UNITED STATES. HE HAD SIGNED A PETITION PROTESTING THE TURKISH ARMY'S CRACKDOWN ON KURDISH CIVILIAN AREAS IN THE SOUTHEAST. MANY OF HIS FRIENDS WHO HAD ALSO SIGNED HAD BEEN FIRED FROM THEIR UNIVERSITY POSITIONS AND SOME HAD BEEN DETAINED. HE DOESN'T SEE A FUTURE FOR HIMSELF IN TURKEY. HIS PARENTS ARE DEVASTATED BUT QUIETLY AGREE.

## Miray

MIRAY, DAUGHTER OF ORHAN AND BINGÜL, IS UNMARRIED AND LIVES IN ERZURUM. AFTER FINISHING HIGH SCHOOL IN ISTANBUL, SHE COULDN'T DECIDE WHAT TO DO. WHEN SHE READ PAULO COELHO'S BOOK, *THE ALCHEMIST,* SHE REALIZED THAT SHE NEEDED MORE MEANING IN HER LIFE. WHEN HER MOTHER TRAVELED TO ERZURUM TO VISIT RELATIVES, MIRAY ACCOMPANIED HER. THERE SHE FOUND A LIFE VERY DIFFERENT FROM ISTANBUL. SHE LEARNED THAT HER MOTHER'S FAMILY WAS KURDISH, SOMETHING NO ONE HAD TALKED ABOUT AT HOME. SHE JOINED AN ORGANIZATION THAT TRAVELED AROUND THE REGION PROVIDING PRENATAL CARE TO KURDISH WOMEN. SHE IS STUDYING TO BECOME A MIDWIFE, SOMETHING SHE THINKS HER CIVIC-MINDED FATHER CAN'T OBJECT TO. HER FATHER WANTS HER TO RETURN TO ISTANBUL, ARGUING THAT WHILE THE TURKISH MILITARY IS FIGHTING THE PKK IN THE SOUTHEAST, IT'S TOO DANGEROUS FOR HER TO BE INVOLVED IN KURDISH ISSUES.